To Myself

TO MYSELF

Notes on Life, Art and Artists

by
ODILON REDON

Translated from the French
by Mira Jacob
and Jeanne L. Wasserman

George Braziller, Inc. • *New York*

First published in the United States in 1986 by George Braziller, Inc.

Originally published in France in 1979 by Editions Corti under the title
A soi-même

English translation copyright © 1986 by George Braziller, Inc.

For information, please address the publisher:

George Braziller, Inc.
171 Madison Avenue
New York, NY 10016

Library of Congress Cataloguing in Publication Data:

Redon, Odilon, 1840-1916.
    To myself.

    Translation of: A soi-même.
    1. Redon, Odilon, 1840-1916.   2. Painters-France-
Bibliography. I. Title.
ND553.R35A2   1986   760'.092'4   [B]   85-26788
ISBN 0-8076-1145-X
ISBN 0-8076-1146-8 (pbk.)

Cover design by John Atwood
Printed and bound in the United States of America

First Paperback Edition

To Myself

◆◆◆

Confessions of An Artist

To Monsieur A. Bonger
in good friendship

I have made an art according to myself. I have done it with eyes open to the marvels of the visible world and, whatever anyone might say, always careful to obey the laws of nature and life.

I have done it also with love for several masters who led me to the worship of beauty.

Art is the *supreme range*, high, salutary and sacred; it blossoms. In the dilettante it produces only delight, but in the artist with anguish, it provides grains for new seeds.

I think I surrendered obediently to the secret laws which led me to form, as best I could, and, following my dream, the things into which I put my entire being. If this art went against the art of others (something I do not believe), it also brought me, however, an audience that time maintains, and even brought me friendships of quality and kindness that are sweet to me and that reward me.

Notes that I express here will help in understanding this art more than whatever I could say about my ideas and technique. Art participates also in the events of life. This will be my only excuse for speaking exclusively about myself.

My father often used to say to me: "Look at those clouds, can you see as I can, the changing shapes in them?" And then he would show me strange beings, fantastic and marvelous visions, in the changing sky. He loved nature and sometimes told me, about the pleasure he had felt in the American savannas, in the vast forests he had cleared, where he was once lost for many days; he told about the courageous and rather wild life he had led there when he was young, venturesome of fortune and freedom.

From the stories he used to tell us within the family, about his former adventures (he had been a colonist, he had owned negroes), he appeared to me an imperious being, independent, even hard, before whom I always trembled. Although today, at a long and confused distance, and with all that remains of him in my eyes, I see in the depths of his own, which easily moistened with tears, a merciful and sweet sensitivity that his outer harshness could scarcely conceal.

He was tall, straight and proud, with great natural distinction. Born near the small city of Libourne, (where several villages and many families bear our name), he was young when he left for New Orleans during the First Empire wars, oldest son of a wealthy family, impoverished by the hardness of the times. His ambition was to acquire a fortune in the New World and return home with the earned affluence which was no longer there.

Many times he confided to us that he landed there without any resources and that, in order to ward off immediate material needs, he had to do all kinds of work, luck always on his side. After he had explored and cleared forests, he quickly amassed a rather large fortune, married a French girl, and some five or six years after his marriage, started to think about returning to France; myself already conceived and close to being born, the second fruit of his union.

Travel by sea was at that time a long and dangerous adventure. It seems that, on this return, bad weather or winds made the boat which carried my parents run the risk of being lost at sea, and I would have loved, thanks to this delay, to have had the chance or to destiny, to have been born in the middle of those waves which, since then, I have often contemplated with pain and sadness from the high cliffs of Brittany, a place without a homeland over an abyss.

It was a few weeks after their return that I came into the world in Bordeaux on April 20, 1840.

I was put to nurse in the country, in a place which had a great influence on my childhood and my youth, and, alas, even on my life.[1]

It was at that time a rather wild and deserted place, and has since changed; I am talking about what was. In those days one

---

[1]Peyrelebade in Médoc.

traveled by stagecoach and even by ox-cart, monotonous lo-
comotion, peaceful, numbingly slow. But spirit free, eyes alert,
we could lie down at full length on the bench of the carriage
and see nothing but the landscape rolling by, slowly, deliciously,
scarcely moving, in a kind of state of contemplation.

Thus, without the noise or excitement of a present-day
journey, and even without fatigue, we could travel the long and
sad road that stretches indefinitely from Bordeaux to Lesparre,
straight and lonely, cutting endless wastelands with its unvary-
ing and high line of magnificent poplars. The view there spreads
up to the skyline over the gorse like an ocean of earth, an
infinity, but without the terror of loneliness you feel in Brittany,
or the desolation of her shores or the melancholy of their
echoes. It seems that in the Celtic air a vast sediment of human
soul has amassed, full of days and of time, like a spirit of things
and of legend as well. The soul sings her choruses which are the
very substance of all her people, of the past and its genius; the
eternal evocation of its torments, and its longings.

In the area I am talking about, which lies between the
vineyards of Médoc and the sea, one is alone. The ocean which
once covered those wild spaces left in the aridity of their sands
a breath of abandonment, of abstraction. At long intervals a
group of several pines, making a steady sad sound, encompasses
and designates some hamlet or park for sheep. It is a kind of
oasis around which placid shepherds with high stilts trace their
strange outlines on the sky. These small villages have no
churches. The humanity one meets everywhere seems to be
annihilated, extinguished and dissolved, each with distressed
eyes in the abandonment of himself and of the place.

It is those arid plains I crossed for the first time as a child
before the awakening of my consciousness, almost beyond my
life itself; I was two days old.

I've crossed them many times since then: oxen were replaced
by horses, and these latter by hard iron on the roads and the
engines of the modern world—I do not complain. There still
remains the spirit of space and of wild places and the harmonious song of the pines under the sea wind, the heather, the
silence and the wonderful burst of light in the bright blue.

9

At the boundary of this heath, running along the beautiful river, stretching narrow and hemmed in by vineyards, is the Médoc with its clean residences, its narrow paths, its luxury of traditional culture where the earth seems to reign over all men, wealthy and poor alike.

Wine, which made her famous in former times, dominates all the hopes of the inhabitants who sacrifice all of their resources and their labor to it. But the wine comes or it comes not. And during the lean years, men remain, nevertheless, subdued by the yoke of its culture. Mysterious domination. It seems that those who attach themselves like this to the earth, under some occult power, work obscurely but beneficially for the necessary duration of her juices; a kind of reward law established without their knowledge and for the delight of human beings.

I bless those who still remain tied to the culture of this liquor of life which yet pours into the mind a little optimism. It is one of the ferments of the French spirit; it is also the liquor of dreams; it exalts to goodness.

In those regions of Médoc, my father owned an ancient estate close to the chateau, surrounded by vineyards and uncultivated lands, with big trees, gorse as always, and heaths. When I was a child, one could see nothing beyond the door-step but wastelands garnished by thorns; the remains of wide rows planted with young elms and oaks; abandoned roads, half wild, formerly reserved for the use of the whole estate: solemn, grand remains; a natural setting, without convention and without lines, generously felled out of the woods of the virgin forest, perhaps, through land nobody measured. After having left my nurse, I was entrusted there, in this old manor, to the care of an old uncle, who was at that time manager of the estate, and whose good-natured blue-eyed face holds a very important place in my childhood memories.

If I question those memories, as far as it is possible to bring back to life distant states of an awareness now dead, and by the altering of its survival, I see myself in those days as sad and weak. I see myself as a watcher taking pleasure in silence. As a child, I sought out shadows; I remember finding deep and peculiar happiness in hiding myself within the large draperies in the dark corners of the house, in my play-room. And outside, in the countryside, what fascination the sky could exert over me!

Later on, a long time afterwards—I do not dare say at what age, for you might then call me an incomplete man—I spent hours, or later the whole day, stretched out on the grass, in the deserted places of countryside, watching the clouds pass, following with infinite pleasure the magical brightness of their fleeting variations. I lived only *in* myself, with a revulsion for any physical effort.

Feelings I had then, and which have left me with distant memories, are those of my games with the little children of the house with whom I was left quite free. A vague period, where my memory does not serve me well, and which would not reflect here many things, except the eternal frolic of childhood, far from the constraint of the city and of its troubles.

I was quiet, not at all a fighter, unskilled in the roving adventures through the fields where the others guided me. I was more often confined in the yards or garden and busy with peaceful games.

Moreover I was unhealthy and weak, always attended to; it had been recommended that I avoid cerebral fatigue.

When I was seven years old, I made a sojourn in Paris, where I stayed for one year, and I remember long walks with our old servant who accompanied me. At that age I saw museums. Dramatic paintings left a strong impression on my memory; in my eyes remains only the representation of the excessive violence of life; only this impressed me.

I said I had a sickly childhood, and that is the reason why I was put into school late, at the age of eleven I think. This period is the saddest and most distressing of my youth. I was only a day-student, yet I recall myself late for classes, and working with an effort which grieved me. How many tears I shed upon boring books, which they ordered me to learn word for word. I think I can say that between eleven and eighteen I felt nothing but resentment toward studies.

These studies were uneven, unfinished, without method, carried out in two boarding-schools at Bordeaux, little Latin. I came to life again and was happy only on the holidays, when I could keep busy. Using the earliest hatching methods I had made copies of lithographs from that time. I have kept several. Those old documents from an earlier time, far from thrilling me, today give me only a shiver, like the repercussion of a distant depression, becoming real through those images.

Nothing particular otherwise.

The great emotion is at the time of my first holy communion under the arches of Saint-Seurin's church; the songs exalt me; they are really my first revelation of art, other than the good music I had already often heard at home.

Thus, it went till adolescence, divine adolescence. State of mind lost forever! I was the radiant visitor of churches on Sunday, or I approached the outside of apses under the irresistible spell of divine songs.

By preference I went into the poor districts of the suburbs, where the temples are crowded, the piety more natural and true. Those are hours when I remember feeling life at its utmost, high and supreme, extraordinary. Was it through art? Was it through communion with the people I loved or through the crowd I still love? Since then, I discovered again supreme joys in Beethoven, but they seem to me diminished by all that humanity collects in it and changes in it: we mix into the Ninth Symphony our own sad joy. This one, born of sacred songs, revealed to me entirely an unblended infinity, discovered like the real absolute, actual contact with the hereafter.

Around age fifteen I was given a drawing teacher with whom I worked on holidays. He was a distinguished watercolorist and very much an artist. His first words—I will always remember them—were to advise me that I was an artist myself and that I should never allow myself to make a single pencil line without my sensitivity and my reason being involved. He made me do studies which he called "nature studies," where I was required to translate only what was dictated to me by the laws of light and statics. He had a horror of what was done in practice. In his analysis of the copies he had me make, he brought a penetrating and subtle sense of the process, a clairvoyance to decompose and to explain them which astonished me immensely at that time, and which I understand today. He possessed watercolors of English masters whom he admired greatly. He had me make copies of them.

As I was very independent, he let me move toward my preferences. He considered as a good sign the tremblings and fever that the exalted and passionate canvases of Delacroix gave me. At that time, in the provinces, exhibitions took place that were open to large consignments of great artists. Thus I could see at Bordeaux works by Millet, Corot, Delacroix, and the first appearance of Gustave Moreau. My teacher spoke to me about them like the poet he was, and my fervor increased. I owe to my open teaching much of the first growth of my spirit, doubtless the best growth, the freshest, the most decisive; and I well realize that it was for me of much greater value than the teaching in a public school.

When, afterwards, I went to Paris to direct my work towards a more complete study of the live model, it was too late, fortunately; the fold had been made. Since then, I have never given up the influences of this first teacher, romantic and enthusiastic, for whom expression was all, and the *effect* an attraction or a subterfuge of art that is absolutely necessary. It is with him that I learned the essential law of creation—I mean the law of construction, its measurements, its rhythms, that structure of art which cannot be learned by rules or formulas, but which is transmitted and communicated only by the union of teacher and pupil in work. The good devil thus took me over. When this meaning was revealed to me, I quickly abandoned myself to the joy of opening my heart through sketches. And it was indeed an effort of reason, of duty, almost of virtue, when I had to set myself to study objectively; I preferred to attempt representations of imaginary things that haunted me and I failed fruitlessly at the beginning. However I made many of them: landscapes, battles, evocations of beings scattered in rocky plains, a whole world of despair, black smoke of the romanticism which still hung over me.

I also made drawings from etchings—these with true pleasure. Should I start again today my education as a painter, I believe that for the growth and the largest development of my faculties

I would do many drawings of the human body. I would dissect it, analyze it, and even model it, to be able to reconstitute it easily, repeatedly, from memory. Of studies of skeletons, I did many. One recognizes the necessity of this science only later. At the age of sixty Delacroix said that if he were to start his career over, he would only study skeletons (this is indeed the avowal of an imaginative painter); he had just come into possession of one for the first time. It is said that Michelangelo applied himself resolutely to the study of anatomy at the age of thirty or forty. What a mysterious adventure to come into the world constituted like this, unconscious of the way one's potentialities would develop, and to provoke in some manner the awakening of his certitude, the knowledge of his own source and strength, through the thousand risks of the influences coming from an environment and time or from formulas of the surrounding pedagogy!

I have kept tender and pious memories of my teacher and of the fervent hours of study and sweetness spent in his atelier (I was fifteen to eighteen years old); an atelier surrounded in profusion by flowers, in a garden out of the city, in the silence of solitude, and under the daylight of a large bay on the edge of a small wood.

Later on, during my visits to Paris and on my way home, I always went to see this beloved teacher because he so obviously adored art, music, beautiful books; he talked about them with a fire that consumed him. But, having withdrawn from Paris and from his weariness over certain disappointments, he again saw me with affection and anxiety. Considering the slowness in which I was held by my fruitless attempts, he advised me to produce much and thus, he said to make "a break through." He thought that at age thirty I was quite late to give first fruit. Perhaps he was right in regard to some others; he was wrong concerning me. I was still trying to find myself at that age.

I was also tied by friendship to Armand Clavaud, a botanist, who later produced works on plant physiology. He worked with the infinitely small. He searched—I don't know how to express it—at the edge of the imperceptible world, that life which lies between animal and plant, this flower or this being, this mysterious element which is animal during a few hours of the day

14

and only under the effects of light. Clavaud was extraordinarily gifted. By nature as much scholar as artist (which is rare), always humbled by the revelations of the microscope, always at his herbarium that he visited, cared for, and classified unceasingly, he passionately devoted himself to reading and to literary research with an enlightened erudition. Thus he could form in the silence, difficulty and isolation of provincial life, a library composed only of masterpieces, those of men of letters of all times. He spoke to me about Hindu poems he admired and adored above all, which he got expensively, imposing on himself privations in his poverty. Very well informed, he kept up with everything. When the first books of Flaubert were published, he already pointed them out to me with clearsightedness. He made me read Edgar Poe and Baudelaire, "Les Fleurs du Mal," at the very hour of their publishing. For Spinoza, he professed an almost religious admiration. He had a manner of pronouncing this name with such sensitivity and softness in his voice that you could not listen without emotion.

Among the plastic arts, he delighted in the calm vision of Greece as much as the expressive dream of the Middle Ages. Delacroix, whose painting still encountered many opponents, was vehemently defended by him; and I can still hear the demonstration he made to me of this sense of life and passion he felt in it telling me the essential irradiation which spreads out from the attitudes of its warriors, lovers or heroes; of the passionate life, in a word, he saw there and which he compared to the genius of Shakespeare, telling me that one word of the dialogues of the English dramatist immediately draws the character of the whole. The same with Delacroix: a hand, an arm perceived in a fragment of the scene expresses also all of the being.

Ah! this dramatic and disproportionate hand of the father of Desdemona that damns! How often had my friend shown me with exaltation this hand, the beauty, the legitimacy of its deformation. The style of this hand in its boldness was, I think, the initial essence and the motive of many of my early works.

I owe to the talks with this friend who was so lucidly intelligent, the very first experiences of my spirit and taste, the best, perhaps, although he considered with anxiety the vain attempts I made, at that time, in my art. Perhaps he would have preferred to see me busy reading or writing, who knows.

Later I always saw him each time I went to Paris. He was my refuge when I returned to Bordeaux. When he died several years ago, I felt suddenly that I was missing a support. His death left me with an uneasiness. I was in conflict, a conflict full of pain and with no way out in the face of the inevitable. I would like now to give him my resolved thought, surer than in former times. About me he knew only the sensitivity of a wavering and contemplative being, totally enveloped in his dreams. He was older than I and his education was strong and solidified by science, in spite of his idealism. And he was like an anchor; I listened to him.

Here are some of his words which I noted:

"The beautiful is free evolution, helped by force (force considered here as positive)."

"The ugly is the victory of the obstacle or the victory of the evil force."

"There is a static element and a dynamic element; beauty can be calm and represent repose, or it can represent movement and life."

"If I say that beauty is the free flight of life, this definition is not strictly accurate, because if I look at a sunset, a magnificent line of mountains, these are not alive in the perfect acceptance of the word. The word *strength* would be more appropriate to this definition, as it is much more general."

"The sublime is an evolution of the positive force mixed with the idea of success, of common good, of justice."

"The apotheosis (or false sublime) is the flight of the human persona in a sense that is personal, selfish, limited to the *self*; it is pure egotism."

"The sublime is altruism; the apotheosis is the opposite."

"There is a subordination in the diverse modes of beauty. A work of art is as much more beautiful as the importance it has in time and space."

"Grace is the beauty of movement."

I am still speaking here about my youth. At the age of

seventeen I started, with little faith and only to please my parents, the study of architecture. I worked daily with an architect who had talent, and also for some time with Lebas. I did much descriptive geometry, piles of working drawings, a whole preparation for the so-called School of Fine Arts where I failed the oral examination.

But nothing is lost in study: I think I owe much as a painter to the study I carried out as an aspiring architect, of the projections, of shadows that an intelligent teacher made me do with meticulous attention applying the abstraction of theory and demonstrations on tangible bodies, and proposing to me, in problems to be resolved, special cases of shadows projected on spheres or other solids. Later on, it helped me: I could more easily bring together the probable with the improbable, and I could give a visual logic to imaginary elements that I foresaw.

Finally I formed myself on my own, as best I could, because in the education I tried to get I did not find the training I really needed.

I made sculpture during one year in Bordeaux, in the private atelier of the professor of the city. There I touched that exquisite soft subtle material which is clay, trying my hand at copies of antique pieces.

Here, at the so-called, School of Fine Arts, at the atelier of X... [2] I tried my best to render shapes; those endeavors were vain, useless, without ulterior reach for me. I can confess to you now, in confidence, after having reflected during my entire life upon my faculties and my gifts, that I was motivated, when I went to the Academy, by the sincere desire to place myself among the other painters, pupils as they had been and hoping for approval and justice from others. I did not take into account the formula of Art which was supposed to lead me, and I also forgot my own temperament. I was tortured by the teacher. Whether he recognized the sincerity of my serious disposition to study, or he saw a timid subject of good will, he visibly tried to impose his own manner of seeing and make me a disciple, or to make me disgusted with art itself. He overworked me, was severe; his corrections were vehement to the point that his very

[2] Atelier Gérôme

17

approach to my easel upset my comrades. All was in vain.

He recommended that I enclose in an outline a form that I saw palpitating. On the pretext of simplification (and for what?) he made me close my eyes to light and neglect the vision of substances. I never could constrain myself to that. I feel only shadows, the prominent reliefs; all outline being, no doubt, an abstraction. The education that was given to me did not suit my nature. The teacher had of my natural gifts the most obscure, the most entire misjudgment. He in no way understood me. I saw that his obstinate eyes were closed to what mine saw. Two thousand years of evolution or transformation in the manner of understanding optics are a mere trifle in comparison to the difference between our two opposite souls. I was here, young, sensitive and inevitably belonging to my time, listening to who knows what kind of rhetoric that issued, nobody knows how, from the works of a certain past. This teacher drew with authority a stone, a shaft or a column, a table, a chair, an inanimate accessory, a rock and all of inorganic nature. The pupil saw only the expression, only the expansion of the triumphant feeling of forms. Impossible tie between those two, impossible union; submission that would lead the pupil to become a saint, which was impossible.

Few artists have had to suffer what I really suffered afterward, softly, patiently without rebellion, to take my place along with the others, in the common line. The consignments to the Salon which followed this teaching, or rather this aberration of an atelier, have had, you can well imagine, the same fate as my student works. I persevered in that blind alley much too long; the awareness of a specific direction had not yet come to my mind. In this distance in which I was left apart from the world I became different from the others and independent. I am, today, quite happy about it. There is a whole production, a sap of art which circulates now out of the branches of the official structures. I was brought to an isolation where I am in the absolute impossibility of making art differently from the way I always made it. I understand nothing of what are called "concessions"; you don't make the art you want. The artist is from day to day the receptacle for his surroundings; he receives from outside sensations and he inevitably transforms them, inexorably and tenaciously, according to himself alone. There can be true production only when one has something to say by necessity of expansion. I would even say that the seasons have an effect upon him; they accelerate or moderate his skill: such effort, such endeavor attempted without the influences that groping and experience reveal to him are fruitless for him if he ignores them.

I believe I have taken great care in guiding my faculties; I conscientiously questioned myself about the awakening and the growth of my own creativity, and about the desire to present it perfectly, in other words in its entirety, autonomous, as it must be for itself. But had I the temperament of a draftsman or of a painter? What is the use of searching for this now? The rather vain discernment that pedagogy has made of those two means is of little importance. However, by analysis, we make distinctions between them. I began to practice drawing later, led by desire, slowly, almost painfully. I mean by the word *drawing*, the power of formulating objectively the representation of things or persons according to their own character. I always strained, by way of exercise, and because it is necessary to evolve in the most essential element of the art that you practice; but I was also obedient to the instigation of the single line—just as I gave way to the charm of chiaroscuro. I also forced myself to reproduce minutely with the most possible visible details and by means of relief, a piece, a fragmentary detail. It was the study that attracted me the most without preoccupation of its use. Those fragments have been useful to me many times since then, to reconstitute entire works and even to imagine others. Such is the mysterious path of endeavor and of the result in the fulfillment of a destiny. For some people it is positive and very determined; it was often disturbing and disquieting to me, but I never lost sight of a more lofty purpose and never resisted attractions I felt coming toward me from other arts. I was a faithful listener to concerts; I constantly had in my hand a beautiful book.

My contemplative attitude made painful my striving to convey external reality. At what moment did I become objective, that is an observer of things, a viewer of nature itself to arrive at my purpose and appropriate visible forms? This was around 1865. We were immersed in the naturalism of the avant-garde; Courbet spread true painting by the palette knife. This unrecognized classic put the youths who were the true painters into a ferment. Millet also jostled the mind of the worldly by drawing the peasant in wooden shoes and the rusticity of his bare and passive life. I had a friend who initiated me by theory and by example into all the sensualities of the palette. He was like my opposite pole; thus endless discussions. Together we did landscapes in which I pushed myself to represent the true tone. I made successful studies at that time which are, doubtless, incontestably painting.

This companion of my independent youth was profitable to me, and life, with its risks, its hardships, its offenses to our tastes by the hard obligation of necessity later took him away from painting. How many others full of natural gifts will be lost and vanish in the same way as so many ordinary men! We are each born with another man inside us whom our will maintains, cultivates and saves—or does not save. One does not know, one will never know what makes this one become an artist, that other a financier or an official, although they had set out together, crowned with the same potentialities. It is an unfathomable, an irreducible point. Fortune or poverty are not an obstacle in this case, the soul is everywhere; you have material at your disposal everywhere. It is a matter of internal bearing, outside of the weakness of vanity or the aberration of pride. There are artists of genius in poverty, there are others in opulence. The end of destiny lies in oneself; it follows hidden paths that the world does not know; they are filled with flowers or thorns.

What had made my commencement so difficult for me and what made it come so late? Could it have been a way of seeing that did not accord with my gifts? A sort of conflict between my heart and my head? I don't know.

The fact remains that from the beginning I always strained towards perfection and, it would seem, towards perfection in form. But let me tell you now, that no plastic form, I mean perceived objectively, for itself, under the laws of shadow and light, by the conventional means of "modeling," could be found in my works. At best, I tried often, and because it is necessary as much as possible to know everything, to reproduce in this way visible objects according to an art style based on ancient perspective. I did it only as an exercise. But I tell you today in all conscious maturity and I emphasize that all my art is limited to the single resources of light and darkness and owes much also to the effects of the abstract line, this agent of a deep source operating directly on the spirit. Suggestive art can furnish nothing without the sole recourse to the mysterious plays of shadows and to rhythms of lines conceived mentally. Ah! have they ever had a higher achievement than in the work of da Vinci! It owes to them its mystery and the fertility of fascination that it exercises on our spirit. They are the roots of the words of his language. And it is also by perfection, excellence, reason, the docile submission to the laws of the natural that this admirable and sovereign genius dominates all the art of forms; he dominates it even in their essence! "Nature is full of infinite reasons which have never been experienced," he wrote. It was for him, as assuredly for all masters, the evident necessity and the axiom. Who is the painter who would think otherwise?

It is nature also who orders us to obey the gifts she has given us. Mine have led me to dreams; I submitted to the torments of imagination and the surprises she gave me under my pencil; but I directed and led those surprises in accordance with the laws of the organism of art which I know, which I feel, with the single goal of producing in the spectator, by sudden attraction, the whole evocation, and the whole enticement of the uncertain within the confines of thought.

Nor have I said anything that has not been grandly foretold by Albrecht Dürer in his etching: "Melancholy." One could find it incoherent. No, it is written, it is written according to the mere line and its mighty powers. Serious and profound spirit cradles us there, like the hurried and luxuriant accents of an austere fugue. We sing nothing after it but the shortened motifs of several measures.

An art that suggests is like an irradiation of things for the dream, where thought also sets forth. Decadence or not, it is this way. Let us say rather that it is the growth, the evolution of art for the supreme flight of our own life, its expansion, its highest point of support or of moral maintenance by necessary exaltation.

This art of suggestion exists whole in the exciting art of music, more freely, radiantly; but it is also mine by a combination of several elements brought together, of forms transposed, or transformed, without any relationship to contingencies, but having, nonetheless, a certain logic. All the erroneous criticism written about me when I began came from not having seen that nothing had to be defined, nothing understood, nothing limited, nothing specified, because all that is sincerely and amenably new—like beauty, moreover—carries its meaning within itself.

The designation by a title given to my drawings is sometimes superfluous, so to speak. The title is not justified unless it is vague, indeterminate and aspiring, even confusedly equivocal. My drawings *inspire* and do not define themselves. They determine nothing. They place us just as music does in the ambiguous world of the indeterminate.

They are a sort of *metaphor*, Rémy de Gourmont said, in placing them apart, far from all geometric art. He sees in it an imaginative logic. I think that this writer has said in a few lines more than everything that has ever been written about my first works.

Imagine arabesques or various windings unrolling not on a plane but in space, all that will furnish the spirit with the deep and indeterminate margins of sky; imagine the play of their lines projected and combined with the most diverse elements, even including a human face; if that face had the peculiarities of the one we perceive daily in the street, with its immediate, fortuitous (*very real*) truth, you will have there the usual combination of many of my drawings.

They are then, without further explanation which cannot be more precise, the repercussion of a human expression placed, by permitted fantasy, in a play of arabesques, where, I do believe, the action which will be derived in the mind of the spectator will incite him to fictions of great or small significance according to his sensitivity and according to his imaginative aptitude for enlarging everything or belittling it.

And again, all proceeds from the universal life: a painter who draws a wall other than vertically draws badly because he would distract the mind from the idea of stability. The one who does not represent water horizontally would do the same (to cite only very simple phenomena). But there are in botanical nature, for example, secret and normal tendencies of life that a sensitive landscape painter could not disregard: the trunk of a tree; its character of force releases its branches according to the laws of expansion and to its vigor that a true artist has to feel and to represent.

It is the same with animal or human life. We cannot move our hand without displacing our entire body in order to obey the laws of gravity. A draftsman knows that. I do think I listened to the intuitive indications of instinct in the creation of certain monsters. They do not depend, as Huysmans insinuated, upon the aid of the microscope before the frightful world of the infinitely small. No. In making them, my greatest concern was to organize their structures.

There is a certain style of drawing that the imagination has liberated from the embarrassing concern of real details in order that it might freely serve only as the representation of conceived things. I have made several fantasies using the stem of a flower or the human face or with elements derived from skeletons which, I believe, are designed, constructed and built as it was necessary they should be. They are like that because they have a structure. Every time a human figure fails to give the illusion that it is going to step out of its frame, as it were, and walk, act or think, there is no truly modern drawing. One cannot take from me the credit for giving the illusion of life to my most unreal creations. All my originality, then, consists in giving human life to unlikely creatures according to the laws of probability, while, as much as possible, putting the logic of the visible at the service of the invisible.

That specific kind of drawing flows naturally and easily from the vision of the mysterious world of shadows to which Rembrandt, in revealing it, provided the word.

But, on the other hand, my most fertile system, the one most necessary for my expansion has been, I have often said it, to directly copy the real while attentively reproducing objects from external nature, in that which it contains of the most minute, the most particular and accidental. After the endeavor of minutely copying a pebble, a blade of grass, a hand, a profile or an entirely different thing from living or inorganic life, I feel a mental ebullience coming. Then I have the need to create, to let myself go to the representation of the imaginary. Nature, thus measured and infused, becomes my source, my yeast, my ferment.

From this origin, I believe my inventions true. I believe it for my drawings; and it is probable that even with the large part of weakness, of inequality and of imperfection itself in everything that man recreates, one would not for an instant accept their appearance (because they are humanly expressive) if they were not, as I have said, formed, constituted and built according to the law of life and of the moral transmission necessary to everything that exists.

To Myself
Journal (1867–1915)
Notes on Life, Art
and Artists

◆◆◆

1867–1868—If by enchantment or by the power of a magic ring you could see what is going on in a small studio in the "Allées d'Amour," between these four small walls which are witness to so many errors and mistakes, so much weariness and defiance, you would be astonished by the novelty of its look and by this entirely new atmosphere of study and work that one breathes here.

If one understands by genius the desire to create so simply, so expansively, that nature itself would be translated to an insane but grandiose degree, I have it.

October 15—I have been in the country for a month; my impression is the same as I always had, for a long time, before the beauty of art was revealed to me. First, a great physical well-being which is not to be disregarded; then an excellent disposition of the soul which influences the character and makes us truly better.

Thus, for the moment I am satisfied; I work.

The isolation of the beloved object renders its brilliance and intensity. It grows, it imposes itself and claims more than anywhere else the law of its *empire*.

Officials consider themselves powerful because they bestow medals, rewards

An artist is powerful when he has imitators. Nobody has received diplomas from the hands of Millet, Courbet, Rousseau, and yet how many painters have received from them this direct and dominating influence which draws them just the same.

There is a book to be made on the *Apotheosis*.

The official painting juries, officiously recommend that you present *important* works to the Salon. What do they mean by that word? A work of art is important according to its dimensions, execution, choice of subject or thought.

The principles of numbers signifies nothing in the judgement made of beauty. All works recognized as good and beautiful by a *single* jury should be admitted. The Salon will not have diversity as long as this principle is not embraced.

◆　◆　◆

How many disillusions in approaching more closely a man of genius! What eternal and inexhaustible illusion the genius maintains in the eyes of other men!

Through the vision of the walls of our cathedrals, as through that of the marbles of Greece or of Egypt, everywhere civilized or savage man has lived, we bring it to life again through art, spontaneously, radiantly and it is a prodigious resurrection.

In short, one must suffer, and art consoles; it is a balm. And the forgetfulness we find in this blessed research makes our richness, our nobility, our pride.

My life detracted little from certain customary habits, the rare moves that I made did not permit me to question any further the laws of my expansion.

Our days alternated between town and country; the latter relaxing me always, giving me, along with physical strength, new illusions; the former, and above all Paris, assuring me the intellectual springboard upon which all artists must exercise incessantly; it gave me above all consciousness of the endeavor of hours of study and youth; insomuch as it is good to be unconstrained when one creates, as much again it is good to know what to love and where the spirit takes flight.

Rembrandt gave me ever new surprises in art. He is the great human factor in the infinity of our ecstasies. He has given moral life to shadow. He has created chiaroscuro, as Phidias has created the line. And all the mystery that art allows is hereafter possible only by him, for the new cycle of art which he has opened outside of pagan reason.

I did not really love painting and my art until—habit formed —after endeavors in several senses, I felt I wouldn't say virtuosity, but all the unexpected and surprising elements that my own creations could give me, as if their result had surpassed my hopes. I have read somewhere that the power of putting into a work greater significance than desired by oneself, and surpassing, in some manner, one's own desire by the unexpectedness of the result, is given only to human beings of complete sincerity, complete loyalty, to those who carry in their soul something more than their art itself. I also believe, that they must have concern for truth, perhaps the presence of pity or even to have suffered.

Would that art might be a stay, a support of expansive life, and would that it might assume that we, who are narrow-minded and weak, need its help! Sublime communion with the entire soul of the past. Grandiose patrimony of a defunct humanity.

◆　◆　◆

May 1868—How does it happen that provincial towns, particularly those which have no museums, do not think of owning a collection of superb photographic reproductions of the drawings made known to us by Braun.

The study which makes a *picture* does not provide resources as durable as the fragmentary pieces established without concern for order or for placement on the canvas. It is not what one consults when working in the studio, and looking for the support of a firm direction. Naïve study, on the contrary, made in the forgetfulness of what one knows, with the desire to approach, as closely as possible, what one sees, remains, inversely, a firm document, rich, fruitful, inexhaustible in resources and of which one will never tire. "Next to an unknown, place a known," Corot said to me. And he made me see pen and ink studies where the leaves were visible there in abundant clumps, drawn and as if engraved. "Each year go and paint in the same place; copy the same tree," he also said to me.

April 12, 1869, Paris—Nature in an admirable law wants us

to profit from everything, even from our errors and our vices; for it is an incessant life, a continuous effort of inexhaustible strength. A single look at us proves life and shows us the accomplished step. What is it in the end but the return of an old man to himself and all the faith he finds there?

There are those who ask what the word spiritualism means. It is they who listen only to their instincts and who take for madness the supreme revelation of poetry. The ideal is a chimera; brightness of truth and certainty of conscience are caused only by the character of our early education and the environment in which we lived.

The word spiritualism will always be understood as expressing the opposite of the word materialism. To define it is impossible.

Beauty and goodness are in the heavens. Science is on the earth; it creeps.

Positive hope in an immediate future endows action with great energy. To act against all hope is to act by virtue.

The Code will replace the Gospel when it becomes the sincere expression of universal conscience.

The day that society, moved by good, brings to the law the spirit of morality and welfare, which presides over individual effort, that day will mark the ultimate reign of freedom and of obedience to the divine word.

In the beginning the ideal touched particularly only a few men; these were the prophets. Their empire was rightful and the divine pressure they exercised on others was fertile and necessary. But days are coming when the unanimity of wishes will make of the law a docile expression of the great human conscience and, consequently, the only prime mover for liberty.

◆　◆　◆

August 18—Let us not be discouraged, let us look a bit at others and we will see that all of them have many tribulations and worries. It is not with gold that we count constantly but with other hardships. We count with sickness, with the world, with time and years; we count with our friendships that fade;

we count with the heart as well; and indeed does it not have its mysterious reasons and its empire which disturbs the most beautiful days? Let us not complain; the hard weight of material life is not the most painful. I wish you dry bread, hard bread, but a happy heart.

Besides, with the years which overtake us arrives a certain wisdom making the obstacle lighter and the work easier. And study and progress? These are the compensations which we acquire for a long time, for always and for self renewal again.

One knows a man by the choice he makes of his companion and of his wife. Each woman explains the man who loves her, each man reciprocally can reveal the character of his beloved. It is rare for the observer not to find between them plenty of secret and delicate ties which will make it easier for him to study life and understand the hearts of others. I think that the greatest happiness will always be the fruit of complete harmony and that the evils of life will be born always in those who have not surrendered. The most loved of the two is the closest to perfection. But a perfect union can only be born in merit; it proves from one and from the other a constant understanding of mutual rights and duties. Herein lies the secret of peace and harmony: outside of that is discord: thousands of confirmations of support for the one who knows how to discern—through the imperceptible tendencies of the heart in this infinite world of aspirations, and desires which animate it—the disastrous waste of lost goods, the remains of the feast and the sorrows that accompany them.

◆　◆　◆

There is something of the heart that withers upon reading pages written too close to human nature. The had part of certain writings is to have laid it open, cynical and abject; it would have been better to have revealed to us what it has of grandeur and consolation.

Writing and publishing is the most noble work, the most delicate one could do, because others are involved. To work upon the mind of another—what a task, what a responsibility for truth and toward oneself! Writing is the greatest art. It crosses time and space, manifests superiority over the others as over music, whose language is transformed also and leaves in the night of time its work of the past.

Your evil is in aristocracy. From the hour of your freedom you fall upon the good things of the earth and vices have accompanied you. Egotism, lust, despotism, sensuality, complete forgetfulness of the general welfare. You have not even a shadow of republican virtue which, however, animated the bold revolutionary, your generous liberators. Are you to blame for all those evils? Who will reply? Liberty in your hands could not suddenly shine with supreme brilliance. The blame lies with the nobility who was the first to deviate; during the days of weakness and doubt you call upon absent faith; you forget that liberty implies strength and weakness together and that this abandonment itself is the proof of it.

Blame, defiance, this perpetual obstacle to the achievement of good, sets the price of our efforts.

When I am alone, I love the wide roads. There, I have conversations with myself. My free steps move easily and my body leaves my spirit free of obstacles; it discourses, it reasons, it presses me with questions.

But with God, as friend of nature, I prefer obstructed paths under the hindrances of a wild road untouched by human work. I let my foot tread the damp earth and the touch of the limb which grazes my face inspires me; stones, bushes, though filled with brambles, stop me only to converse with me and speak to me; and even in a black, very dark wood, I love the storm, the plentiful rain, the cold, the ice and snow; all the frost, the wintry weather of which people complain, has for me an eloquent language that attracts me, charms me and has always profoundly enchanted me.

Plastic art is dead under the breath of the infinite.

Lucky are the wise men for whom life is self-controlled and whose strength is in balance with desire. They dominate us regardless of the mediocrity and the inferiority of their understandings; they judge us, they prevail over us because they do not fight. A quiet life is a deserved one. The noble have it; let us not be jealous of it. Their great assurance, by living in leisure on their fortunes, shocked only well-born souls; they have honesty, dignity and even goodness; their manners are exempt from petty bourgeois preoccupations. But their error does not lie there. They are guilty only of the egotistical mistake of supposing that people are incapable of sharing feelings that only they can have; and also for having given throughout history this fatal example of luxury, excess, and personal anticipation, the consequence of which, this taste for well-being, is one of the traits of our epoch. People could only imitate what they had seen; from there, their torment, as they have not yet their own tradition. Leisure, repose, reflection, the salutary occupation of reading had not yet put a little of the ideal into their lives. The worries of thought had not yet made those souls feel the nobility and the dignity of life. Could it have been otherwise? Only angels could have sacrificed to live out the first days of liberty.

There is silly laughter that reveals the heart and lays bare the hidden depths of the soul. There are others that reveal celestial joys.

A man of action is not ironic.

The end of a full day brings the mind infinite rewards. The supreme leisure of the elite souls is entirely in those exquisite hours following painful and fertile effort. There is an age when the balance of strengths assures us of sweet celestial joys, the most glorious of life, and the only ones which give us the right to say that we have lived.

◆　◆　◆

1870—Repentance is a new innocence.

Each day which goes away carries its pain; it lifts a little the veil of the truth. The hardest is to see friendships grow cool or extinguished; they are often lost by the nothings of life which separate men in ideas, in occupations, in habits, in pleasures; only friendships of childhood are more sure, and it is very comforting to lean on them. "People" means many things: there are those who look higher and who suffer; they are asking for a little rest. Pain is speaking; they are silent. The best of their feelings is in the depth of their soul, and in their eyes wet with tears you see only goodness.

There are also people who blame scholars, thinkers and wisemen; these are the newly rich, and even kings themselves.

One judges others relative to oneself, comparing them to oneself, instead of considering them in relation to the truth. This man is full of faults that his friends do not have; this other, exalted as if he were an angel, will never meet his social obligations. Opinion is written nowhere.

The utmost superiority of Jesus is to have made *himself* loved without dispute. His legend magnified only his beloved virtues, brought only to the memory of humanity the candor of his smile or of his gentle constant love for those who came close to him.

◆　◆　◆

We live by customs alone; in the usual forms of politeness, which are nothing but appearances of friendship, of goodness, one hides a pitiful emptiness. If so much care and so many false practices are necessary in men's relationships to make society durable, nothing is more hideous than a friendly exterior that hides hate.

◆　◆　◆

What distinguishes the artist from the dilettante is only the pain that the artist alone experiences. The dilettante looks to art only for his pleasure. It is painful to complain to those whom you love. The spirit of justice surpasses goodness. Yet there are hours, hours of love and grace, when in order to give, in order to love, one would gladly be unjust. I never could determine for myself which one is better, the one who gives? the one who justifies? There is matter for much reflection.

Shall we ever arrive at the certainty, at the sense of having done, having given everything? One is walking continually in doubt mixed with confidence, and these dispositions alternately hold the thread of one's life.

And the world and most of those whose hand we hold see the practice of an art as merely a matter of relaxation and of rest!

The taste for art is nothing compared to the caring for the heart. In every artist there is a man, a human being who must be looked after and cultivated. The man is perhaps simply the process for the artist's work. Art is powerless to render the nuances of those situations and all the delicateness of their influences.

The artist should not, by sacred authority, think himself so much above others. To create is something indeed, but it is not all. A mediocre man, or even one entirely without any sense of beauty can very well reveal lofty and very noble degrees of awareness.

Indeed, we should be thankful to heaven that we live in a world where Beethoven and the god of art spread life, and above all, we should be proud of being able to understand it; but I find deeply egotistical and mediocre the very personal suffering of those who, for this reason, would excel over all others.

The world is full of fearless talkers and blasphemers; the harm they do is only to themselves. For me the only real misfortune, the only real torture is the spectacle of false authority that imposes itself. I bear a grudge against those who by their credit, their position, by the authority of a promise improperly acquired, open to naïve souls the first joys of goodness and beauty. I resent all those who, under the arches of our temples, make heard injurious outcries against good; those who martyrize genius; those, finally, who, in the field of awareness, falsify and pervert the natural meaning of truth. These are the truly guilty. Here lies the evil which must be exorcised.

Positivists cannot love modern beauty. Its music is closed to them, except for living, dramatic music.

I have known some with noble hearts, simple and touching by their good nature. They have generosity, quietude, something which resembles the feeling of a duty fulfilled. They have a part of the truth but they do not have truth.

It is a fertile and necessary law that takes us to what we have not: we love what completes us. Art, morality and justice lead to better ends. The error is in trying to discover the poet's formula. Nature is too diverse in her infinite activity to make it possible for us to see through her action and to understand her processes. The heart, love in its delicate gentleness, is still the best and only guide. It is perhaps only through it that the truth is revealed, it has the touch, the certainty, the affirmation.

If a vague, perpetual regret is mixing with every hour of your life, if it persists and obstinately forces itself into your thoughts, your actions, your free time, your will is but wasted power, your duty is not completely fulfilled.

One is proud of the first intimacy with things of the spirit; those who have seen of beauty only the pomp, the exterior, all that is without inner beauty, have more love for them than for her. They speak with emphasis, they enter the Church to be worshipped by it. This preoccupation with their own person is the sign of their inferiority.

What *remains* and what must be known of the *grands siècles* are the masterpieces. They are the most complete, unique and true expression of those times. The most essential, the most characteristic works of the human mind that remain from other periods is better written in second-rate, inferior documents, which are closer to the people, the true artisans of everything.

Any behavior which allows your neighbor to believe other than your thought is a lie. Any act with a concealed motive is a lie. Silence itself, in certain circumstances, might give rise to ambiguity. Where, then, is loyalty, where is sincerity?

The common error of fashionable people is to believe that the world ends with them. A simple inopportune word, a gesture, an attitude is enough to conceal you. The masses are seen by them only as far as the skin.

◆　◆　◆

June, 1872—Of all the moral situations which are most propitious for art or thought, there is none more fertile than the great patriotic sorrows. It is, in fact, the supreme quarrel between peoples so diverse in their aspirations and in their tendencies, that create preoccupations of a much higher order in the individuals who compose them. When they are resolved by arms, that is, by risking death, each of us has in some measure made a sacrifice deserving his moral elevation. Those generous distresses therefore surpass, from on high, the narrow and confused zone of our personal concerns and direct our sentiments toward a better end. They lift hearts, illumine consciousness, stimulate will, develop intelligence. The words humanity, country, honor, duty recapture for everyone their true sense. Finally, they remove mental activity from particular deeds in order to elevate them toward more abstract and more general ideas.

In confirmation of these reflections one can see that the most important artistic movements and our greatest blossoming have closely followed our victories and our disasters, and that in the intimacy of our social evolution, at the very heart of our happy or unhappy country, the era of progress and faith has followed on the heels of the solemn and decisive hour of our supreme revolutions.

An attentive observer could see at that hour, in the creations of thought, a new character which reflects in a certain way the moral state of the country.

You have propitious and supreme kindness. You will give life to those who approach you by elevating the mind, the heart and all it desires.

Exquisite creature, happy and charming, your approach is delicious and inexpressible, it makes you better and more confident, more infinitely docile and tender.

Must we tell you that we love you? Ideal inclination, more pure than tenderness and its surprises, which persists in the memory of charms so young and so pure, invincible as those of angels. It is the timid emotion of reserved adoration, it is candor, the chaste love that is as much like a brother as a fiancé.

Oh youth, oh heart's inclination, supreme and mysterious aspiration of souls toward the pure heavens of goodness, you are the mark of future life. There are in your cautious ecstasies and your mysterious aims all the promises of the invisible, like a support in the unknown. Go ahead, lean incessantly toward that which makes us believe, leads us to our goals, to life, there are only blessings at the hour when you invite us.

♦ ♦ ♦

During the solemn days at winter's end nature, at rest, is immobile. At this intermediary pause, the breath of death and the first fruits of life, the hours have a solemn greatness. Silence, and ultimate surrender, prepare us for the awakening ahead.

Nothing appears yet, everything in the air is cautious: in the highest treetops, heaven's songs reveal nothing of their tenderness. The sun in its violent harshness shines without warming, it falls on the slender branches with a brisk ardor that burns them. The earth in its sadness takes on morose tones, and nothing yet reveals what will be tomorrow.

In these gloomy days of silent spaces, the spirit is isolated. The soft impression that gives way to intimate impressions produces only abstraction and terror. It needs confidence, the hope of a tomorrow.

♦ ♦ ♦

It is repugnant to see at the bar and before the judge a black-robed ecclesiastic who testifies against a guilty person. The sad clothes he wears, his austere mourning is very ill-suited to a temple of human justice that acts only on us and by us, by our passions and our ardor in the struggle, our vengeance and our hardness.

Jesus never accused. He only died for us, with forgiveness and forgetfulness on his lips.

Virtue changes form; it can exist in resistance.

The refusal to do evil, complete isolation at certain hours, can be a beneficial action. One is unjust toward those who practice it, men of *action* and of exceptional will.

The great originality of the *Internationale* is to have said: nobody shall possess. There is the supreme vow, sublime vow of humanity, which turns its gaze away from earth and begins to feel itself on wings.

♦ ♦ ♦

1873, Saint-Sylvestre—There is always a certain solemnity in that exchange of vows and hopes that we form incessantly on the eve of unknown days. In this there is also a certain consoling sweetness at finding ourselves together after many rapid days, when the anguish has not been too intense, and when they gave hope for better days to come. One would hope the coming days would finally be restful and constantly joyful, but wherever one goes, wherever one thinks and exists, one is still in the presence of life, facing the same evils and the same weariness.

This last day ends as the first begins; the life of the heart fills it and commands it.

May 7, 1875—I am at Barbizon. I have here, near me, the forest which cradles its high peaks. I want to know and to understand it. And then rest and forget the feverish life of the city where I tired myself out during this year's winter.

But all effort brings reward, I see it well. Here I have several friendships which are dear to me. It was the small circle of Mme. de R. which attracted me in the evening: four or five aging or old men, two or three intelligent young women and several young men. The former knew the greatest illustrations of 1830 and through them I have new information on those whom I have admired. Delacroix, his person, his character, this is what captivated me in their recollections.

◆　◆　◆

What a pleasure to read in a quiet room with the window open onto the forest. I came back to old Dante, he will no longer leave me. We are moving toward a serious friendship.

I have just reread the letters of Sévigné. She will be my friend at certain hours, what a charming spirit: "My daughter, I let my pen trot." Or again, "I went walking silently with the moon."

Reading is a resource for the cultivation of the spirit. It allows for this silent and tranquil colloquy with the great spirit, the great man who has bequeathed to us his thought. But reading alone is not sufficient to form a complete spirit with the power to act with sanity and fortitude. The eye is indispensable for the absorption of the elements that nourished it, just as they nourish our soul, and whoever has not, to a certain extent, the faculty of seeing, seeing correctly, seeing true, will only confer a partial understanding.

To see is to spontaneously grasp the relationships between things.

July 3, Quimper—One hears distinct steps and echoing noises outside. All is brief and precise. The lively and sudden burst of everything that moves, strikes the eye and the mind like an arrow. Here is the north, falling; here is the sky obstinately lowering itself, heavy and hard, on the men it overwhelms. It rains, a strong mist falls slowly. All is sad and as if oppressed. All of nature, men and landscape, seem to feel the weight of the depths of time. It is the obstinate bondage, the fatal element of the outdoors which keeps everything in chains, on the earth, in the somber sojourn of a stricken country. What a strange terror, what a hard sadness which slowly falls on life and things and which freezes the most protected heart. What is there to do here, to see and to feel, if not to listen slowly to the restless creatures and their voices and their rapid steps. Sad country crushed under dark colors; what a virile and hard stay you offer to someone who is tired by a hard and restless life! You are not a country made for dreaming.

They ask me my certitudes—in art. You must have the good sense to acknowledge, without sentences and without fooling anyone, that you can be certain only about the painting that you have been able to do. All others reside in the power of the unknown, in the mystery of the potentialities of those who will give birth to them.

My *Credo*, then, seems inscribed in what comes of the works that are the fruits of my personal endeavor through all the atmosphere of pedagogy, official or not, from the time in which I have lived, simply.

It is vain or spiteful to domineer.

◆ ◆ ◆

Peyrelebade—Soulac, Soulac, is the expected cry finally heard by the traveler seeking the unknown beach. At first he sees nothing: a large moving carpet of sand, large pines on the sinking dunes. He is alone, almost lost; the native, astonished, approaches with surprise. A few rare bathers will also be there, to see the new arrival or friend. One is so alone there *at the ends of the earth*, it is the only impression you will have of this country half-dead and wild, without life, without culture, almost confined to the Ocean.

You hear it nearby and it attracts you. The sea is here, magnificent, imposing and superb with its obstinate clamor. Imperious and terrible clamor, it makes strange remarks. The voices of the infinite are before you. Nothing of human life. On the high horizon not a vessel, a sail half concealed, is on the wide Ocean. Over there the distant shores of Charente spotted by a few white, imperceptible dots that are houses. Here, the immense beach, undefined, of which the edges are mingling with the sea itself, with the day and the light, with the moving brilliance of the silvery wave.

Painters, go look at the sea. There you will see the marvels of color and light, the sparkling sky. You will feel the poetry of the sands, the charms of the air, of the imperceptible hue. You will return from there stronger and full of great accents.

Poets, go and see this beach. You will have to sing the mystery of infinity. On these shores you will discover intense solitude.

Musicians go listen to its harmony. All of you, finally, who are tired of wordly life, all of you who are oppressed by the weight of days, all of you who work unceasingly in the womb of our miseries, all you men of the fields and humble people—go and breathe in the strength and faith of fertile nature, our mother and friend.

There are certain matters of the heart which have to be experienced and explained in silence.

They come, they go. They leave deep pathways. When time has touched them with its shadow, they are then like an enlargement of ourselves; increased life, a supreme addition wherein we feel divine torment magnify us; where sensitivity, yesterday arid and quite dry, comes back to life, to its former resonance, the living freshness of its first years; its sacred germination which could induce in us the idea that nothing from the heart could ever be finished—*maybe*.

The will has no power over them, at least on certain days, from time to time; that is the most disturbing problem that a moral man has to resolve. It is the most disquieting question that a mature mind, anxious to quietly obey its own law, straining toward perfection, tortured by the will to behave well and with no other aim but to deliver unblemished the accumulation of its morality—has the misfortune to ask.

◆　◆　◆

"The heart has its reasons". It has them, it pursues them, it deliberates in us according to secret, infinitely mysterious laws, so that on meeting a woman—chance meeting—it takes possession of the entire person, it is domination, invasion, an obscure failure where one no longer clearly discerns what behavior is, where the notion of good and evil no longer exists, or is no longer necessary, because what is of the heart at that divine instant is something of eternity.

◆　◆　◆

Already, for having said this to myself, I feel a sort of lull in my sadness; as though the law of loving incessantly produced and created everywhere it appears, a delicious potion, a charming mirage, voice, ecstasy and delirium, where the sky itself opens and is created by it.

◆　◆　◆

A few minutes of her presence, made of what I felt the most delicate, the most tender of woman and women, reverberate in my heart by the maturity of my mind, as if in her were resumed what I have loved the most, what revealed to me the most light, what dominated me the most and attracted me toward beauty.

Woman is our supreme forerunner.

* * *

Each man should be the historian of his own heart. He would be reflected there, he would look at the imprint left by those sweet testaments, instantaneous or slow, always involuntary, which have led us, by dark, dim ways, toward other lights, ever and constantly renewed, toward the lightness of spirit and of the greatest beauty, where the last steps of life, by divine election, reflect the echo of the child's emotions. None of those tender emotions will be erased, and I praise them and consider them, today, as the experienced history of an almost religious and blessed emancipation.

* * *

It can happen then, that in an approach—produced by chance or by the unknown—who knows, spontaneously, sharply, unconscious capture, one is bound. Imperceptibly, at first, without knowing himself already conquered, led, docile, in the subtle joy of submission.

The first day marks the preference; the next day upon awakening, nothing but a glance exchanged, a presence felt anew, the sound of a voice that gives to all chords of the sensitivity a new resonance; everything will be told, clearly revealed. And the need to make oneself known, to tell all, to pour oneself out to her, to tell one's life, to give oneself up, to surrender, to teach her everything she does not know, as after a long separation when it is important that each know—in two beings who form but one—the emotions of pain and joy that the friend must share.

There will be nothing left in order to know in depth the grandeur of the mystery leading us on the night of certainty which melts us, destroys us, leads us astray and fills us with delight, but to know the infinite pain of separation after having been together for three days. There will be nothing more to know than the immense emptiness left by her absence.

Despotism makes man perverted or makes him suffer bitterly. Without the constant effort to protect his life, the free soaring toward the good, he falls inevitably into fraud, lies, and, even more, into contempt for all common good. If he refuses and resists, he will suffer in his chains from the sterility of his skill and if he loves his country and humanity he will suffer for all as he suffers for himself. This is why the love of liberty lives only in great hearts.

Merit and true talent are rare. One must appear to have them in order to inspire confidence that will give us our authority and prestige. Such is the cause of the real lies that society imposes on the man who wants to be able to move freely. This position is acquired only thanks to the sad necessity of pretending we know a great deal even when we know very little.

We do not come together by having the same qualities: this one might possess genius and have, as friends, those whose qualities of heart surpass their mediocre abilities. How charming are goodness, kindness, indulgence!

One can eternally separate those who love, but the ideal will always reunite them.

Nobody will enter into your hopes: dreams, desires, projects are weak and solitary abstractions that nobody will formulate with us. In his aspirations toward the future or beyond it, man is unhappy because he is alone, all that he sees, all that he is, makes him suffer, except for what he loves.

If I had a son to direct, I would tell him: "Leave, go alone in the midst of men since you must become one of them. The individual soars only in liberty."

◆　◆　◆

May, 1876—Without being and willing to be of any sect, of any school, especially in the matter of art, there is a loyalty of mind which must praise beauty everywhere it is found and which imposes on the one who understands it the desire to communicate it, to explain it.

I am not *intransigent*. I will never extol a school that,

although commended for its good faith, limits itself to pure reality, without taking into account the past. To see and see well will always be the first precept of the art of painting; this is a truth of all times. But it is also important to know the nature of the eye that looks, to seek the cause of the feelings the artist experiences and communicates to the dilettante—if indeed there are any—in a word, to discover whether the gift he has made is of good nature, or well woven; and it is only once this work of analysis and criticism has been achieved that it is important to put the finished work in its place in the temple to Beauty that we have erected in our mind.

In the crowd, one carries within the willfulness of destiny.

◆　◆　◆

Good sense is the ability to judge well, even without any training and on an order of truth that is a little "down to earth." This ability is highly useful for men who have to deal only with the most immediate realities, the imminent ones. It is indispensable to those who make art; therefore, its absence can sterilize the most precious gifts of the best spirits.

Nevertheless one can totally and ridiculously lack common sense and have genius. So be it!

But the painter always has an eye, an eye that sees.

◆　◆　◆

1876—Photography used only for the reproduction of drawings or bas-reliefs seems to me to be fulfilling its true role in helping and assisting art without leading it astray.

Imagine museums reproduced in this way. The mind refuses to calculate the importance painting would suddenly assume if it were thus placed in the sphere of literary power (the power of multiplication) and of its new security assured in time. . . .

◆　◆　◆

I feel an aversion for those who pronounce the word "nature," with their mouths full and their hearts empty.

I see such people, at the height of their age and talent who have nothing but their *style*, impotent practice, sterile habit, torpor, vain desire to show themselves as skillful. They disregard the studies of Corot which are masterpieces of awkwardness: the eye and the spirit in them command everything; in them the hand is a slave to observation. Corot is the ingenious and sincere initiator of that painting style, just like that of painters of former times when they studied.

Landscape done in this way interests me and attracts me like a delectation. To think that industry has taken over the studio model: one can find in shops pieces of casts, the entire nude made lifelike: the result is truly deadly. It is as ugly to look at, as a plaster cast from nature.

For the landscape the same cynicism: trees, forests, streams, plains, skies, clouds. One could do no worse than falsify our view, corrupt students, kill the seed of any art behind young brows.

Rembrandt, in spite of his masculine energy, maintained the sensitivity that leads through the passages of the heart. He investigated all its folds.

Etching is an agent quite different from accurate photography. It does not make inferior the piece it retraces or recreates; it is not superior to it; its purpose is different; it is something else.

Any documents of emotion and passion, of sensitivity or even of thought left on marble, on canvas or in a book, are sacred. There is our true inheritance, our most precious one. And with what nobility it clothes us, poor and precarious creatures that we are: the slightest chronicle, the most precise date, a simple human fact, could they ever tell what the marvels of a cathedral reveal, the smallest shred of stone from its walls! Touched by man, it is steeped in the spirit of the time. Thus every age leaves behind its spiritual age. It is by art that the moral and thinking life of humanity can be felt again and recovered.

If we could gather and make appear suddenly the immense chain of materials on which man left all the pulsing pain or joys of his passions, what a sublime reading it would be!

If I had had to speak of Michelangelo on the occasion of the centenary, I would have spoken about his soul. I would have said that what is important to see in a great man is above all the nature, the strength of the soul that animates him. When the spirit is mighty so is the work. Michelangelo spent long periods of time without producing. It was then that he wrote the sonnets. His life is beautiful.

There is, in Amsterdam, a painting that is still in the house where Rembrandt had seen it and placed it. The nail that rivets it is still the same one the Master set in, in the very place and under the light he had chosen. In France we are incapable of thus preserving a work of art for such a long time in the same place.

Music is a nocturnal art, a dreamlike art. It reigns in winter at the hour when the soul is confined.

Music shapes our soul in youth and later we stay faithful to our first emotions; music gives them a new life, a sort of resurrection.

June 2, 1877—What is called natural, grace, the full and sweet soaring of the human person is a sign of his freedom, of his superiority. What is revealed by a true attitude, by harmony, by the beauty of free movement, comes from the very depths of life. All exteriors reveal a soul; they explain it, they prove it. But when I fix my eyes, even for an instant, on any being in real life who moves easily and harmoniously by the laws of supreme balance, I cannot help, at the same instant, but feel myself live highly and mightily. This elevates my spirit, and makes me think.

I contemplate the same thing in the universe; the great Being so certain, so present and mysterious, whose secrets upset me. I see it in all of nature, on this day which is so full, so pure, the first day of spring. My heart soars towards it; higher and farther to the depths of the firmament, my eyes are lost in it, fixed on it.

I feel myself proud and strong in my conscious vision. External things which are brightening unceasingly around my anxious person today strengthen all my will. I feel myself a man, at last a man in his plenitude; in me life amplifies to excess and to its fullest, it palpitates. Sensitive to everything, everything speaks, and the word has never been revealed this clearly, so loudly, to my astonished eyes.

There is a conscious goodness, a goodness which is strong and equal, which considers itself as the idea of good it is practicing. It is born of understanding as much as of the heart: capable of constant kindness, endless, it is the sister of duty, it is human justice with its height, its scorn, its love and its hardness.

There is a natural goodness, a goodness weak and soft, inexhaustible. A goodness which spreads always, without regrets or returns, which finds its source in all things: this one is a gift of God, the former comes to us from men; this one is the sacred blessing, which spreads goodness and life everywhere; it is a celestial seed which sprouts everywhere and spreads life, and the only good here below which gives us the right to say that we have lived.

The poorest and the humblest of women, the sad and lonely woman, the one in whom fear is epitomized, the pain of rags, in a word, the weak being forgotten by the world, will always be the charming and sacred one who deserves to exist, who has the right to a tomorrow. Only if life had withered her soul, would she have no more charm, mildness, or beauty.

I have always loved poverty and the dignity of rags. My heart would have to be quite low to remove my faithfulness, my support and my tenderness and I don't know a weakness more miserable than that which turns us away from a human creature who stretches his arms toward us, offers us his smile, forgiving us for what we have usurped from him.

◆　◆　◆

August 10—One could not write without the concern of maintaining one's thoughts every day, every hour, in the presence of things and of life. The universe is the book which we read incessantly, the unique source, the means. It is not enough to train only our minds; it is also necessary to polish one's constant reflection and follow with vigilance the austere discipline imposed on every brain that strives to expand and produce; outside of that, there is no style that is one's own and that reveals us to ourselves, like that of the great prose writers.

My purest friendships are among you, poor children who live in the streets, who sink in the fields under the rays of the burning sun or under the hardship of icy winter. I will leave life pleased to have understood your sweet smiles and the infinite charm of loving you. Love me as I love you. *Never,* not for a single instant—I say it from the very depth of my soul—never have I committed the slightest injustice toward you. I am ready to give you the purest of my strength, to help you and share with you the difficulty of your labors.

To watch your purest natural talents die, one by one, to watch them fall, forever, like the green branches pruned from the tree that cannot support them; isn't there perhaps a law of necessity which diminishes us in order to assure our life. Time carries us quickly; the days of a man are hardly sufficient for him to realize even one of his faculties! Who would ever be able to see in this infinite world of love and active revelation, which raised the heart of the gods of art, which knows their beginnings, before their generous hands had shaped the treasures they have left to us! Oh youth, divine ardor! How many things fall from you into this obscure and incomprehensible nothingness, and what efforts, what labor later, to retain still virginal and fruitful a single one of the gifts you left for us!

You must not smile; only anger is taken seriously. He who sustains injury without regret is misunderstood and unknown. One must strike, one must beat. Usurp in contentment, beyond this is madness. Return the blows I make you endure, or you are not one of us. Strength kills. Our love is for it; and if you search higher, any adventure through happiness or dreams, what good is our support? Thus speak the worldly people, enemies of the lonely.

Abominable situation, where a just spirit can find its place only in sorrow! Everywhere the same irony. The closest are the hardest. Not a word of confidence, no sympathy. It seems that he who goes alone in search of truth and who is exhausted searching for his method, the law of his striving, can only find support by reason of his inferiority and the vulgarity of his inventions. The day a page of Dante elevates and affirms us is

49

the day we are shocked and wounded. You will not be more than I am, thinks your fellow man who sees on your forehead the trace of noble reveries. Then he scoffs. Stupid and brutal will the contempt you endure go before you, like all that is invisible? Will the pain you communicate leave in you the best of you and of your soul? Will you feel finally that your role is the lowest? The one who suffers is the one who rises. Beat, beat again. Wounding is fertile.

To judge does not mean to understand.

To understand all is to love all.

◆　◆　◆

Around 1877–1878—*Letter to a friend*

"Good sense is the ability to judge well even without any training and along the lines of rather down-to-earth ideas."

It is supremely useful to people who deal only with the closest and most immediate realities of life—it is of little use to those who look beyond. It is sad to state that its absence can sterilize the most distinctive strengths of the best minds. With originality one can console oneself for not having any. But one can be completely ridiculous and without common sense while being a genius.

What did they do to cultivate their spirit when there were no books?

They looked at the universe and at the earth. And, in the reading of this work, men formulated the most moving chapter: they saw themselves living, they saw man as now, at the center of an infinity, whose mystery was no more or less impenetrable; and in the relationship of men with nature they discovered, nevertheless, certitudes and in a certain measure, faith was thus possible, thus ardent, the very element that makes us think we exist.

All sensation makes one think. Reading is an admirable resource for the cultivation of spirit because it modifies us, perfects us. It allows this speechless and tranquil colloquy with the great spirit, the great man who has bequeathed to us his thoughts. But is is no less true that reading alone is not sufficient to form a complete spirit able to function with sanity and strength. The eye is also indispensable for the absorption of the elements which nourish our soul, and whoever has not developed in a certain measure the faculty of seeing, of seeing correctly and truly will possess only an incomplete understanding: to see is to spontaneously grasp the relationships among things.

I send you these short pages, a mere trifle which made me dream for a few days. It is under the spell of our autumn evenings that I have again taken up these remembrances. This time of year favors a return toward the past; it is sad and recalls that which is no more. It creates in the soul a silent murmur as discreet as falling leaves and the tempered light of the day.

◆　◆　◆

1878—Why was it not until after the war of 1870, at a late age for others and an age of renewal for me, that several clairvoyant friendships came to me?

I frequented a group of cultivated young people among whom I had a childhood friend: Jules Boissé. It was a cerebral home, an elite, one of those radiant centers, with no interest in power, searching only for art, beauty, good, and which was later disbanded by the death of some and by the progress of others towards leisurely thinking or dilettantism.

The great intellectual ferment came from the utterance of Chenavard heard at the house of one of his students Mme. de X. But alas, this great doubter, this disappointing analyst, illumined the chamber with a miner's lamp. Quick to contradict but never affirming, sharp at guessing, there came out of his false talks a sense of irresolute weakness. He propagated scruples which generated the sterile destruction of effort. But his speech was substantial. He also related anecdotes with rapture and subtlety. His talks were a book open on the men of his time, all of whom he had known, compared and weighed. I used to ask him in particular what memories he had of Delacroix. What he told me of him communicated to me a fervent faith in creation.

All that was told to me of the life and tastes of this great and passionate artist awakened my instincts, made me free and brought to my quest a fervor without torment.

Chenavard told me that he often walked with him along the banks of the Seine, near the high walls of Notre Dame, in this solitary place well-suited to meditation. His friend (Chenavard), reasoner, researcher, bewildered by theories, conversed with him on art, on the masters, and could not convince him of the approaching end of humanity. In spite of the fine and inspired conversation of his companion, Delacroix sometimes told him, "Chenavard, don't speak any more, I don't want to listen to you at all." And yet, his illustrious friend related to me, when his eyes perceived in a shop window an engraving of a master he loved, of Rubens, of Corregio, then he would himself begin to speak brilliantly, and it was his turn never to finish. . . .

He almost always worked standing up, alternately moving away from and approaching the easel, whistling or singing an air by Rossini whose music he greatly liked.

A painter friend of his, unknown today, had the power to influence him a great deal. This most independent spirit was sometimes intimidated and willingly entrusted his palette to his friend, leaving to him the task of making himself, on the canvas, any correction he advised. But after only a few retouchings, Delacroix was unable to stand it any longer, tore the brushes from the hands where he had placed them himself and reprimanded his intimate collaborator with the most biting and witty epithets. And he returned to his original idea. In public, in society, the same modesty. We know that he praised the classical writers.

Greediness—foolishness maybe—ardor or an unbridled passion for success or for rising in the world have degraded the artist to the point of perverting in him the sense of beauty. He uses photography directly and shamelessly to transmit the truth for him. He believes—on good faith or not—that the result is adequate when it can only offer him the lucky accident of an unrefined phenomenon. The negative transmits nothing but death. The emotion felt before nature itself will at all times supply him with a much more authentic amount of truth, controlled only by himself. The other is a dangerous communication. I was told that Delacroix had recommended it: that greatly surprises me. The statement needs to be verified.

◆　◆　◆

May 14—Gustave Moreau is an artist who has not and never will have all the fame he deserves. The excellent quality of his mind and the subtlety of his practice of the art of painting gives him a particular place in the world of contemporary fine arts. He produces little, or at least it appears to be little, judging by the rarity of his exhibitions; but he always produces with certainty, with an assurance of talent which marks someone who knows clearly what he is searching for, what he wants. The vivid and sparkling watercolors which I call historic watercolors, reveal him entirely and strongly, making a new charm visible in his manner which is a little rigid, a little tight. The *Phaeton*, in particular, is a work of great scope. I don't know what memory of Delacroix's superb sketches comes over me as I behold this brilliant page whose daring and originality of vision could be coupled with the creations of this master. Delacroix has more abandonment, more abundance; the power of his imagination has carried him toward the most varied subjects of history; above all, he has more passion and the supernatural light which falls on his entire work sets him apart and very high on Olympus. But I see more excellence in Moreau's research, an exquisite and delicate penetration of his own consciousness as a painter. He knows what he wants and wants what he knows as an accomplished and impeccable artist. He is like the writer who chisels his form without losing any of the soaring flight of his ideas. An admirable logic guides the progress of his imagination.

This *Phaeton* is a conception full of boldness; its objective is the representation of chaos. Has anyone ever imagined anything like this? Who knows; nowhere has the plastic representation of the fable been formulated with such an accent on truth. There is in the brilliance of the clouds, in the audacious divergence of lines, in the harshness and bite of the vivid colors a breadth, an emotion and somehow a new astonishment. Look in the numberless illustrations of the fable for someone who has interpreted this one as he did; I defy you, if you have entered for one instant the cold vaults of the academic temple, to find there a mind that rejuvenates antiquity in this way, with such an entire liberty and in a form so contained and, at the same time, so vehement.

This master (as he is one, if we have to give this title to those who demand of others as well as of themselves the full flight of their originality), this master has never left, since the very outset, the legends of pagan antiquity, and constantly presents them in a new light. This is why his vision is modern, essentially and deeply modern, in that he concedes, above all with docility, to the indications of his own nature. Let us admit that the life in those works is an artificial and false life about which nobody cares.

Little has been published on the art of drawing; books, brochures, so abundant on all other subjects, are almost totally lacking in this particular area. Popular curiosity, and a more and more pronounced interest inspire reading, but there are only very rare opportunities to be informed on this subject. Except for some purely esthetic treatises or other works which give a general view of the schools and of beauty—works which speak only to minds already cultured or specialized—the public, which likes rapid reading, finds there but a few things to glean, only on the occasion of annual exhibitions which have been recently organized in the provinces; in the daily newspapers he can then skim through analyses of what he could observe himself. But this kind of writing which is based on current events, does not allow those who publish them to deviate from a particular matter whose purpose is not didactic. Besides, the critic thus placed between the beholder and the artist often feels himself closer to the latter by personal preferences and ideas which could be without any significance for the former but of a non decisive influence.

The only articles capable of giving wings to thought are reviews, the new form of the book, where some distinguished minds sometimes treat more general questions. But this sort of publication does not fall under the eyes of everyone, only the specialist cares about them; whereas the less subtle amateur, for whom art is a luxury and who only deals with it in his leisure time, cannot benefit from them, except when the articles of the review have been gathered and grouped and put into the more durable and more determined form of a book. But these books are lacking. Few thinkers have turned their thoughts toward the arts; and let us quickly add that the militant publicist, the one who addresses the public daily, does not care very much about it either.

The reason for the great abandon of the art of drawing is related to general causes which would be too long to enumerate here.

◆　◆　◆

It is in winter that music has its greatest magic, it is especially pleasing in the evening, in harmony with the silence, to delight the imagination it awakens; it is the art of the night, of the dream, but painting comes from the sun. It is born with the day and the light, and that is why, always at the beginning of a season, at a time when the landscape painter goes to the fields, the Parisian dilettante prefers to turn to the art of color and life, like a gentle rest after the winter and the long evenings.

◆　◆　◆

Truth, action, the art of producing living people, such is the *ne plus ultra* of literary creation. It is not common in Germany, that country of dream, music and abstraction. But in France, but in England!

◆　◆　◆

It seems that all the musical vigor of Germany has stopped its heart at the Atlantic shore; England has no music. She has followed the literary branch; and as she is the nation of passion and life, she has given us this astonishing pleiad of poets and men of letters which surpasses in richness and variety the productivity of all other nations.

55

◆　◆　◆

The translation of a literary work makes it lose its flavor, its perfume; the essence has been placed in another cup. It is like a nectar which has evaporated and lost its scent.

Journal[1]

First day—I have loved three times during a few hours. Women, here, are the strangest and most terrible creatures; they torture the less sensitive heart: grace, abandonment, pride, genius, here are the supreme strokes of these incomprehensible beings such that it is so painful to love and so hard to forget. The naturalness and passion of the children are adorable.

But this place of light and space enraptured me. I saw for the first time your airy suspended snows, oh mountains, I am under the brilliance of your immensity. Your slender peaks pierce space and penetrate the azure to depths without end. Oh ravishing feast, how many things there on high for him who suddenly sees you, lively, just after having left the dingy and banal city: here one feels the epic, the poetry; our soul is a mere trifle—the first stage happy and rapid. Tomorrow is a holiday; charming people, I will see you again.

Second day—The day of Jesus, but banal and without poetry. Day marked however for thinking of the sweet comforter of the poor; a thousand prayers, no love, not a single act in his name; a struggle, a clash of contrary ideas. The memory of the great heart who dreamed of justice and the reign of the ideal vanished in broad daylight. Banal and sterile day that speaks of those who have and those who have not.

Your hills from which the eye sees infinity, where the sensation of our own infinity penetrates us, even here the heart needs

[1]Journal written at Uhart (Basses-Pyrénées) in 1878.

support. Solitude gives to love a vehement stubborn intensity. Isolation from the beloved object makes its brilliance and its strength. It reigns, it imposes itself, it takes possession of the least sensitive heart. The most rugged of sensual pleasures would be to possess in a desert the being who is the most sacred. The joy that could come in bringing together two souls would be infinite. There is a power of happiness which can be attained only here. Oh women, oh mountains, which world is the greatest? One would reply according to the days and the time. At twenty those summits persistently plunged me into rapture; ten years later, I remained more tenderly cradled at the edge of the clear waters that bathe their roots. In the shadow of these green hills, which in former times I have seen withered by winter storms, I felt the desire to meditate; I saw on a smaller scale and more deeply. Is it weakness? Who knows? Wings do not belong to those whose gaze is no longer raised toward space. There is courage and goodness in resting one's eyes on friendly and lively nature who assures us that in our future we will have less mind and more love in all that comes directly from the best of us.

I came down from these green hills to go to the plains; and these first moments of admiration have changed imperceptibly. To the extent that my vision turned away from the sky, it rested on man. So that in ten days I made the trip from the realm of dreams to that of reality. Perhaps there exists in life's resources, a mysterious and consoling rule which has us descend into human intimacy as we leave outer intimacy.

It is strange that the strongest impression I gather from this country of vast horizons is an impression of love. I finish and sum up these days by elevating my mind to the mysterious and charming being, whom God placed close to us for our joys and our sorrows, and I venerate with emotion everything that comes from the heart when it is simple, silent and confident. It is a sensual pleasure, subtle and touching, to try to reach characters through the varied outer appearances of human conditions. That of the poor is the most attractive and among them that of young girls: who are the most affecting and the most gentle. For everyone there are also particular predilections; perhaps we have intimate ties with places on earth where we have lived. The

Basque country is for me like an ancient fatherland where I must certainly have lived, suffered and loved. There is not the slightest breath of its breezes, the slightest sound of its waters, the simplest of its charming voices, which does not awaken in my heart unintelligible harmonies and something like the recollection of my cradle. All that comes from it touches me and exalts me. I will long retain the fleeting impression of this short stay. I hope that good fortune will take me back again to those places, to reunite me with those among the poor who are dear to me.

Third day—It is a pity to see the loss of a certain grandeur in our traditions and our heritage. Estates and castles and even remote names, famous in our history, no longer have greatness or good bearing. The sons of the middle classes, prosaic and common, dispose at will, without religion or poetry, of those precious remains which can, so easily, stimulate the desire to proudly and firmly take possession of them. But it seems today as if they were only in transit; they are not at home. Most of them live within those dark and high walls, just as if they were in an inn that they will soon leave. They talk about art to put us on the wrong track; the wish for equality is the tomb of thought; they say it without understanding it at all; they do not see the very works that others bequeathed to them. They trample on beauty; their rough hands scratch the inspired canvas that their stubborn eyes would not be able to see. Without any decency they put their hammer to the panels of those antique walls in order to fashion them for their own use, thinking that in this way, they are living with originality; without realizing that with an irreparable weakness they are being ruled by the morals and actions of those who cried out more loudly than they. This banal expansion of sordid wealth, without the instinct for lofty matters, inspires in others a true judgment. Those are the real poor, the only ones whom it is right not to help. The rich are those who are eager for truth, who are filled with understanding, and with gifts of the heart.

Eternal misery for some, illusion for others, painful encounter between those who believe they can console themselves in life by occupying much land, and others who are searching only for ideas and who lose themselves in this search on the way to truth.

Printing is such an important event that we are still at its advent; the most distinguished mind can be taken by what is so new and impressive in the molded and multiplied letter. This is the cause of so many grievances and injustices and also the reason for the sudden attention paid to the publicist.

However, this writer more readily forgives those who do not bring their work to completion. They seem to me to be in the same state as the newly wed whom you meet after six months of marriage: marry, he says, marry, should one not be married?

The authority that somebody else has over us is not dependent on his position nor his renown. It comes spontaneously at first sight to the one who submissively feels his superiority.

The great natural epics of formative times have a larger part of beauty than other poems of the *grands siècles*.

In them live the soul and divine aspiration of an entire generation. Epics are the great monuments of humanity; purely literary works say much less; translation already takes away some part of their beauty; they are restricted and limited in time; and for this reason deserve only secondary importance.

As for the individual epic which is artificial and more strictly literary, it says little and has not much chance of enduring. If it were removed from the literary shelf, history would not lose the most indispensable of its documents.

Fourth day—A small town, people at their doors watching. Shutters are closed and one feels eyes peering at you. What miserable sadness in this life which flows away between four streets, surrounded by vacant people who spend their passion and their life talking about others! What a constraint, what a dependence for the person who elevates his mind towards lofty subjects, and how the most insignificant garden in full solitude has its value! You will be bored there, some will tell you, you will be quite alone there—amuse yourselves poor, sad people of this world; spy, watch, be on the look-out, calculate well; life which flows this way carries you to death after a long torment;

liberty is not for you. It is wherever you can think in peace without hindrance, it is wherever fools and wise men go to listen to the strange sounds that you do not hear, on the banks of running waters under a talkative and hushed sky; wherever nature, if she can see us, contemplates us; wherever she inspires, consoles and enchants us. She is not at your door or behind your shutters where the obstacle of opinion is forged.

Beautiful sky and superb countryside which yesterday enraptured me; forgive this oversight of your eloquent splendors and of your consoling speech. Surrounded by this infinity I quite forgot the true life, that which comes from you.

Sixth day—Bohemians, poets. They are strange, heroic and legendary. They arrive, vanish like people who live nowhere. They give way to an immense unknown growing of which you feel only motivation through the depths of the ages. One feels small in comparison, pitiful and timid. A haughty laugh mixed with contempt and protection receives the contribution that I put into their hand, held out to me without baseness and almost childishly. They quickly walked away, without turning their head, with none of the curiosity which animated us, they rushed away like a bird in flight. At ten paces they already had forgotten us.

One cannot imagine possession when one is at the foot of the mountains. Enclosures on these steep slopes, fertile and rich, what a mere nothing—they cut down the tree at the edge of my field; I will complain, from this there will come a dispute. And the two human creatures lost like an atom at the foot of that immensity forget to see this and to search for higher thoughts inspired by the contemplation of their own petty part. An hour of meditation at the summit of those high peaks from which vast plains unfold, where fields and gardens are lost like imperceptible dots, confers at once the sense of the infirmity of their role and their power and of the equality of powerlessness so evenly spread. Upon returning it will leave in peace the poor fellow who has taken the tree at the threshold of this infinity. Besides, here one is everywhere and nowhere. One is in the unknown, in the unoccupied primeval forest. It seems as if the secular tree which shelters you belongs to everyone and to people of all times. Robbery does not exist here, or at least the feeling which dictates it is different in the plain. Here the law should prevail, differently than in other places. The malefactor himself, if he is ill-intentioned, might even be obeying wilder, more natural instincts than in a civilized place where each man's personality would be more vividly felt.

Tenth day—On what do we lean? On human nature. Two deep, soft eyes captivate us and suddenly we are in love. We would give our blood to possess this new heart that is open to us forever, and the greatest bitterness is indeed that which comes from the harshness of a world that distances us from the beloved and desired object. What becomes of these attractions? They live, they persist, they go away into the infinite. Yes, the heart needs the soul and the soul calls for immortality.

Without this support of the unknown what would we do on earth? The lowest being, bewildered, abandoned in the bleak anguish of isolation, and the tears we must shed to comfort ourselves. Oh truth, mysterious painful and encouraging as that of sudden immediate sympathy, revealed without error! How cruel is the constraint that shatters it, or takes it away, and the greatest pain is that of love without hope; I suffer, and an infinite torment destroys and consumes me; I suffer an obstinate complaint which often penetrates the memory of self and which sums up my best days.

Dear and vast country, which I admire, and which moves me so much, you, whose low sky caresses and consoles me; you, whose deep clouds and green hills almost bring me the memory of a happy childhood in a world where happiness and inno-cence are unknown; you take weakness from my mind. The mournful sound of your waters today speaks of death and melancholy; awake in me strength and confidence.

Oh sadness, infinite grace, secret and aristocratic ardor, lofti-ness, pride spreading out from your wounds; there is strong confidence to be found at the very source of this pain, when it is gentle and without anger.

Oh mountains, the small man climbing you is lost in your immensity, you will never be divided; your domain belongs to all. Your borders, so high, so close to those beautiful clouds, that caress your highest peaks, are next to the sky, where everyone can be inspired and uplifted. Mountains and clouds, region of both the ideal and of dreams.

◆　◆　◆

July 20, Harlem—It seems to me that I am at the end of the world; my writing here is feeble, in the inevitable sadness of one who just arrives. I feel a childish fear in this morose country, half-dim, full of silence, where the moving sky creates uneasiness. And also I have the instinctive defiance which comes to us on foreign soil. Why must I say it? It has been twenty-four hours since I left it, and I already have a devouring, consuming desire to hear French. I would have retraced my steps half-way here if the train had not carried me, in spite of myself, through swamps, waters, seas, boats, and above all, windmills repeating themselves, as far as the low, monotonous horizon. The landscape which unfolds here before my eyes is well known to me; I saw it many times at the Louvre in the Gallery of Masters; in the foreground, on rich grass, thick and of strong color, animals graze on the damp soil; in the distance, some ponds, some trees half-submerged; then the mast of a ship which excites a little surprise as it travels this way over the prairie, slowly being towed; then windmills, always windmills turning full sail, all invariably pointed in the same direction under the ever present and rapid wind. Man appears very small here; he is lost in the thick, turgid atmosphere, without the great picturesque role of the house, the path, the animal or cloud, always swollen with rain, but full of beauty. All is broken, swaying without visible outlines. The only outline of this landscape is in the rigidity of the unique and horizontal line which cuts the picture in two, and extends indefinitely before you, around you, with a force not lacking in magnitude. It is unfortunate and sad, holding no interest whatsoever for the eye; no pomp, nothing from the outside which could elicit astonishment, fertile and durable as in the largely decorative regions where paintings are born at every step, with their frames, their lines and their planes. My greatest surprise was in Rotterdam, the most grandiosely pictur-esque city in these unfortunate parts; but still her beauty belongs to that particular order of things that is out of the ordinary, where nature forces herself on man or asks him only for his support outside of his condition.

Imagine a floating city where you lose the feeling of the ground and its security. I crossed it by day, but its image remained within me like a dream, where bristling masts of vessels and high windmills mutually yield to a lively struggle. Their big wings pointed and turned around in the sky, along streets or bridges turning on invisible pivots; yes, shifting bridges which make way respectfully before the boat, which is king along the walks of this city. The railway crosses it, or rather, is ingeniously laid out on the roofs, so that from the top of the train, you can see this panorama, so rare and extremely gro-tesque, of a modern city in the midst of water and bearing a railway. This spectacle makes an impression on the mind like an aberration of nature itself and predisposes one to reflect on man's power here. Everything in him denotes an extreme superabundant energy. The heads that I observe, from the depths of my forced silence all have a vital glitter unknown in a French country; here, one acts slowly with a vivid will. Peculiar breed, powerful and good-natured, grotesque in some way that I understood and do not like at all. But I have a presentiment of the poetry of these domestic customs and all that lives behind the taciturn brows of her children.

❖　❖　❖

July 21—I hurry to painting and I find life: entering this room of the Academy of Haarlem, where three hundred heads are looking at you with such keen fervor that I thought I was in a crowd from former times, when Frans Hals was alive.

This extraordinary painter has here eight canvases which represent him totally, from his beginnings right up to his astonishing end. His maturity came late, when he was about forty, maybe older, and the works of his old age are additions resulting from an unbelievable degree of organization which, so to speak, does not want to weaken. If ever genius proves that nature proceeds by exception in the case of genius, it is indeed here, in the presence of those supreme and last works created before he died and in no way diminished by the hand of an eighty year old craftsman. It is here, like a vision of painting which will be born two hundred years after him, through the eyes of the French contemporary realists, decadent, if you like, but new, no doubt.

This excessive singularity of extreme art brought to light so far from Paris, this refinement in vision discovered two centuries before us, gives rise to extreme surprise, as if places and time did not exist for the genius. Art is a flower which opens freely outside of all rules; it particularly disturbs, it seems to me, the microscopic analysis by aesthetic scholars trying to explain it. The study of races, delicate study of temperaments and their fusion in a nation could perhaps provide a peremptory explanation, in an irrevocable way, when one speaks about Rembrandt, Shakespeare, or Michelangelo, those prophets. Frans Hals who is not one, is, however, the most powerful man, who knew how to translate animal life into paroxysm.

◆　◆　◆

July 27—I see the Hals works again, this time they seem to me thousands of feet beneath Rembrandt who is high as a mountain. Life and life again, but only animal life. I ask questions of those heads, they say nothing to me, I see them living the life of animals; my strongest recollection today is that of the trustees painted by Rembrandt, probably recalling the works of Hals with which he was probably familiar, or which he had doubtless seen.

Only in his last period, does Hals seem to me to have achieved superiority. Was it the weakness of his hand, was it the diminishing physical strength of this excellent workman; there is in the works of the last years of his life a very marked softening in the execution; but what astonishing ease, what scorn for detail, what power in seeing quickly and finally, and with great scope, the true reality. There is an eye there of which one senses the paroxysms of power. Toward the end Hals is a Master. He has, moreover, at this point, a charming relationship with some French contemporary painters. Was there imitation by these latter? No. It would be necessary to establish a comparison between the diehards and those works: one would find there all that is legitimate, sincere and new in the research of the French realists.

Otherwise, on the whole, this museum also impresses by a Spanish side of its character which has never been noticed: those halbards, standards, plumes, picturesque felt hats, those wealthy and aristocratic fabrics remind me of scenes depicted by Velasquez.

There are around me figures in full bloom, of a freshness of complexion so fine that it awakens the desire to paint. All these heads living and palpipating around me stand out against a dark background of a brightness and richness unknown in French countries.

◆　◆　◆

Amsterdam—*The Night Watch*—A little disillusion. However, upon inspection, charm comes into play. Life, so intense in Hals, wrongs him; nevertheless, the superiority of his genius prevails; in some parts of the picture, on the right, it is superb—the dim parts have darkened, no doubt; perhaps the dimensions of this painting surpass the perfection of the plastic making abstraction of the sum of full-blooded life. Seen in Hals, this painting has a deep and strange charm—all that is in half-shadow is better than the figures in the foreground. What could be more understandable in all the work of this master! Once again, in some places, there are heads, which, seen from afar, take on a magnificent magic. Magic is the proper term—the quality of light is enchanting and supernatural. Except for two or three prominent figures, the rest is magnificent.

The *Syndics* is more perfect than *The Night Watch*, the design being less elevated. It is the most beautiful Rembrandt that I have seen.

◆ ◆ ◆

No one master has painted drama as Rembrandt did. Everything, even the smallest sketches, involve the human heart.

Rubens has a genius for staging.

◆ ◆ ◆

August 5th, Antwerp 1879—Shall I dare to confess that Rubens speaks a language that I do not understand! Certainly *The Crucifixion* reveals the mightiness of this spirit in its largest dimensions; I do not believe I have ever seen such an overflowing of action and truth of gestures, attitudes, expression and variety of expressions as that included in such a vast subject; never has such a rich inventiveness put on canvas seemed as intimately sustained by the depth and touching beauty of thought; people, hangmen, thieves—one of them superb in brutal force, children who are always graceful and charming, as one sees them among the good people of Flanders; women entirely natural and true in the beauty of which they are unaware, like this infinite Magdeleine you see below the cross, with the legs of the divine dead on her young shoulders, and whose deep pain would have me say here that Rubens knew how to paint Goodness; all this subjugates and enlivens me, I feel that I am in the presence of a high level of real creation, and yet, I resist this genius: something absolutely contrary to me keeps me from understanding him, from loving him.

Rubens, let us say, is a master of decadence—one cannot say this about Rembrandt—he belongs to the period of decline of the art of former times, because he has done nothing really new or novel. He is a fiery genius, full of fervor and ideas, who sowed his wild oats throughout his time over the walls of churches, in palaces, among courts and princes of whom he was the friend and favorite; he did not suffer—nothing indicates the long and painful martyrdom of giving birth to a new ideal. He is not a colorist—this could seem a paradox—but I will not say that those same reds, those same blues, all this, in some way stereotypical, illumination of each object, each fabric could be his chief title to fame. A simple grisaille by him contains as much as the finished work. It is because right from the beginning he casts the key idea that he has in mind of the scene he wants to paint, he shows it all in one stroke, shaped in its size, its mass, its truth: he has understood the crowd, he has seen it; he painted Pain, Goodness, Grace, the forgotten Beauty of children and women; he touched, I do believe, the most sensitive fibres of the human heart; he has, no doubt, all the supreme strings of the eternal lyre on which great men have made heard the disquiet of our destiny; he has all this, and he has not the slightest feeling or taste for plastic representation —he has neither the line, nor the plan, nor the simplicity, nothing of what makes for a wise, clear and simple representation of things. In this respect he is related to the English school; he seemingly generalizes nothing with the line, of which he seems to be unaware—I mean the straight line, the one that is active and decisive and without which the shape as well as the painting has no structure. He draws, constructing each object and each person with great vigor; he has an admirable knowledge of the play of all the muscles of the human body. In this he is modern, as he paves the way for the northern painters who, like Delacroix notably, express the life of things much more by reflecting on external nature as they remember it than by observation and analysis directly from the model.

He has all the greatness, all the gifts, and their richness, but he has not experienced the grief of suffering—this is perhaps the only reason for my refusal to place him among the greatest.

In the temple of love that we raise in our mind to the great men, there are two cycles, two distinct places that it is important to separate carefully: in one are the greatest masters, here they are, alone and suffering, overwhelmed by the weight of their deep misfortune.

What are the limits of the literary idea in painting?

It is well understood. There is a literary notion as long as there is no plastic invention.

This does not exclude invention, but any idea which could be expressed in words is subordinated to the impression produced by purely pictorial touches, and in this case appears only as accessory, and finally, as superfluous. A picture thus conceived will leave in the mind a lasting impression that words could not translate, with the only exception of words in the form of art, a poem for example.

In a literary composition there is no single impression. The effect is contained uniquely in the ideas born from it, which occur above all, through memory. In this case there is no real work of art; a narration is worth more; it is pure anecdote.

Example: there is an expression other than simply plastic in the *The Angel Gabriel*, of Rembrandt; the diverse ages of life and the manner of feeling the miraculous, are they not rendered with an infinite delicacy in that old man who falls, as if swallowed up by some divinity; in that adolescent who admires but also analyzes, watches, questions; in that woman who joins her hands in prayer; in that other older one; and, lower down, in the dog who barks and seems to represent the beast in his fright and fear?

Those nuances assuredly belong to the domain of literature and even of philosophy, but one feels strongly that all this is placed here only as accessory and that the artist who has thought in this way, willingly or unconsciously, has not made of them the unique condition of his painting. And the evidence is that all this research, so touching, so naïve and so profoundly deep as well, does not appear until after a long analysis, and that most of the beholders struck by this marvelous work were under the power of an impression which did not come from there; the unique accent of his sublime composition is in the supernatural light which illuminates and guides the divine messenger. There, in the pure and simple nature of the tone and in the delicacies of the light and dark is the secret of the work in its entirety, purely pictorial invention, which embodies the idea and gives it, so to speak, flesh and blood. That has nothing to do with anecdote.

Almost all masterpieces of the Renaissance express a literary idea and, among French painters, often a philosophical one. Art that is uniquely pictorial is inferior, and it is not without justice that Holland and Spain have neither the brilliance nor the magic spell of Italian art.

◆　◆　◆

Dimension — Its relationship to Subject

One can see in the greatest masters an exuberance of methods of which they seem unaware. Their strength carries them too far; often, they go beyond the material limits in which they should frame their thoughts: the exaggeration into which they fall most easily is an excessive size of the painted or drawn surface. Before or after having found the exact measure for the representation of their subjects, and even simultaneously, they go beyond it, they are unable to restrain themselves. It is a genius which expands and produces abundant but mediocre fruits.

This is what Dürer did in wood engravings so large that they were destined to decorate rooms, rather than books. Rembrandt, in spite of his genius for etching, could not resist trying very large plates; and it is easy to see how far those are from the perfection that sparkles in the regular size plates.

Since painting is obviously less limited than etching, it is even easier for painters to let themselves go with the charm and appetite to paint on a large scale.

The most perfect works were produced in a size recommended by taste and reason: but those sizes which a mediocre artist finds easily, seem, by the most inspired, to be due more to chance than to their awareness.

It would be interesting to try to find out which works were treated as having an absolute fulfilled size, and to see at what degree of expansion they were brought forth by different painters.

With Bresdin the same extravagance: he creates pen-and-ink drawings, but next to such beautiful works one can see others which would gain from being treated on a smaller scale. On the stone he does not restrain himself either: in the large proofs, there is no longer any relationship between the fineness, the delicacy of detail and the entire surface which the eye must envelop.

He is infinitely more beautiful in the small lithographs where his genius, essentially minute and profound, expresses itself rationally and finds accents in harmony with the aesthetic and plastic demands of his work[1].

◆ ◆ ◆

1881—A group of several sublime barbarians who arrived from *Tierra del Fuego*, proud human beings, haughty, cruel, mighty and grotesque gave me almost a dream of primitive life, a nostalgia for the pure and simple life of our origins. I never felt with such force the distance our own nature creates between the crawling beast and our highest goal. They carry the marks of our dignity; it explodes in their eyes and gestures with more vigor than in civilized man. It is the animal in the complete mightiness of its instinct, the certainty, the uncorrupted beauty of its modelled form; for they are cast in antique bronze, those limbs so firm and so fine; delicate joints complete those perfect extremities where not a single jewel sparkles, not a single error is visible.

And yet for the person observing them it is easy to understand the relative state of their perfection; they get together and speak softly, mysteriously, as if afraid of being surprised in the secret exchange of their ideas. They undoubtedly speak only to say things which are of the utmost importance to them; the way they look at us expresses as much superiority as wildness; furthermore no fear appears in it. This one stretched out on the ground, his chin on his two fists, follows with his eye, quite far, a civilized man who passes by. In the disdain he feels, his curiosity does not inspire him to make any more effort, for he remains immobile and turns his glance toward another human object within his reach, without either body or head moving.

A rich financier, probably the owner of the garden, enters the scorched circle which encloses them. The savages look obstinately at the red ribbon which decorates his lapel, while I compare them. How ugly he is, this old bourgeois; and they beautiful, these sublime children of polar life! Their nudity

---

[1]Written during a trip to Holland

emerges from the earth like a flower of India, in full bloom, luxurious, harmonious and immobile in the splendor of its radiant and mute life. One must see that rigid flesh framed in lianas, in the shadow of the virgin forest, or lying on the golden sand of the desert, on immaculate shores.

What poetry is an organism so perfect, coming from primitive nudes, to stammer out next to us the first stanzas of a universal hymn!

◆　◆　◆

May, 1885—*On a bronze by Marie Cazin*

Oh regret! of which the living image is seated on a rock, like an incarnation of eternal melancholy! Where do you come from? Your figure leans over the abyss. Your finger on your closed lips and your hand on your heart, you kneel like scattered leaves.

Would you be the symbol of lost glory? Would you be solitary meditation? Would you be piety, silence, dream, care? Would you be the contrite face of the black pessimism of this world? And under your fatal and obstinate brow would you be concealing forevermore gloomy motives hidden in all things? Perhaps these lips will open only to tell us that your heart suffers and those green branches, emblems of strength put at your feet, will suggest to us that all is vain.

Be that as it may, work of mystery, you warm my heart with the true sun of art; a recollection of Florentine visions pursues and obsesses me since your desperate profile turned toward the lowly conceptions of the contemporary worker.

Around you like dead figures surge mournful evocations, silent and wan, whose emptiness and insipidity serve to raise your majestic bronze still higher.

In the isolation where your metal shines, do you seem to say also that in former times masters were great and their aims higher; that they could live for an art of sincerity; do you seem to say that Passion surpassed talent, alone showing free souls the source of beauty?

But false seers worshipping false gods told us, nevertheless, that people elsewhere were submitting to magnanimous influences.

71

They told us that a school held the secret of style, the science of rules, the book of the way; sad pride shown for a few rigid lines well traced, for those grotesque busts so well aligned, for that stone chiselled without life, for those icy marbles made no one knows how, nor by what industry, and which recall only death.

Marie Cazin, previous to this art, started with beautiful drawings of a rare simplicity, sketches of stark improvisations which foretold of tendencies to statuary; firmness of contour, simplicity of plan, sobriety of subject, rhythm of lines, all bordered this austere art, notably the *Sleep* whose strong and simple expression accentuated the striving toward the goal, achieved today with the appearance of the *Masque*, Marie Cazin's first cast.

Since then we have kept before us the unforgettable brilliance of this metal face, which seemed to come from another world. It was the same sadness, the same intensity of feeling, the same infinite contemplation; in one word, the resurrection through bronze of the *Interior dream*.

June 12—I passed along the cold and silent paths of the cemetery next to deserted tombs. And I found peace of mind.

Death, here, under my feet, in the dark graves where friends and dear ones rest, at last, happy because they feel no more; death here, certain and coming so soon, hovering over our worrisome days as the only balm for our miseries; death here, mistress and always sovereign, forever; I have seen her, divine refuge, happy end of the evil of life.

Oh death how vast you are: for you I cry; others call and question you. In the calm that the thought of you gives me, what strength against misfortune!

Oh divine unknown, mute face, fear without name, majestic immobility, how great is your beauty! Men religiously decorate your sacred field; here are flowers on your stone, art, decorum, ceremonious worship; on the marble of the mausoleums, large and lofty thoughts for all times.

I feel in these places other than myself.

In Morbihan I saw some superb places, but they were so wild

that I left them. I am now on the shore of a delicious bay which would be even more charming if the sun could embellish it a little more. For only one day was I able to see this country as one would like to see it, under the positive influence of a little light which tempered its harshness. Otherwise, until now, all I have known of Brittany is an eternal fog, a dim and changing sky drizzling, buffeted by contrary winds; and of the ground, alas! nothing but a clump of sad and slow things which fall on the mind and oppress it. No, this country is not mine; it is *sad* here. I will stay here nevertheless to explore some fine rocks of which I have been told (and indeed, I have seen some really unusual ones); but I will hurry to the South which after this will seem to me to be a fairyland.

Beautiful, peaceful ships, gently lifted by the eternal wave, you float in a friendly harbor. Your long leaning masts and their thin ropes strike the depth of the foggy sky and the breath of the air and the rhythm of the waves cradle the spirit like a gentle harmony.

You hurry suddenly to reach the bay; far and wide, the last ship has lowered the solemn sail and the breath of the air and the rhythm of the waves cradle the spirit like a gentle harmony!

In the harbor is a festival; they have seen you from afar; here is the woman, here is the wife; the virgins who, two by two, speak softly on the shore. And the breath of the air and the rhythm of the waves cradle the spirit like a gentle harmony.

Beautiful, gentle ships; so dear to the sailor, what do you carry in the depth of your skiff? From the bosom of the Ocean, to the immortal source, fishing, treasure, the catch was so great. And the breath of the air, and the rhythm of the waves cradle the spirit like a gentle harmony.

Oh sea, oh great friend!

August—Jules Boissé died of peritonitus in eight days as though by surprise. I had been called late, the day before; but he was still fully conscious, with all his intelligence occupied by his death. He was not very sad at leaving life; one could see that in his irony. We conversed softly that night, a hotel room night, heartrending with abandonment and distress. The noises of the boulevard rose and sent us the songs of students on a spree that disturbed his rest and he said to me smilingly: "I do not envy them. . . ."

All that night he seemed to me to be anxious about the cause of my presence near him, although he was tender, he wanted to believe only in my curiosity! "You have come to see me die," he said, when he saw me entering the room. "That is not interesting. You see, I have all my analytical awareness (these are his own words) and I am the advance of decomposition; I have no more than six hours, as the unconscious molecules of my dying are at work. The hiccups that you hear are in spite of myself; I do not suffer, thanks to the injections of morphine they have given me, it is like sleep. I die worn out, perhaps by mistake, perhaps by 'social impossibility'."

He could not allow others to pretend not to understand the seriousness of his state at that hour! So much knowledge and clairvoyance in a moment like that is frightening. What is the grace which helps us go through it, with such great courage?

Whose turn is it now? Death lives in my mind because I have *seen* it. It will be as destiny decides. And all that is not cheerful.

◆　◆　◆

May 6, 1887—It was in May. After days of endless apprehension, incessant uneasiness, for I have never had a birth happen near me (neither my brother, nor my sister, both unmarried, have ever revealed to me the adorable marvel of birth.) New, therefore, to this anxiety, on a hot and humid day in broad daylight, I watched my son Jean being born.

I loved him immediately. At the very moment of his life, which I sensed was fragile.

What a little thing he was, and human! And in my heart what pity! I think I can say that all paternal love depends on this supreme instant, when life is revealed to us in its most pitiful condition. It is in truth over days and months the infinite weakness of the being.

He had eyes imbued with nocturnal brilliance, a delicate

mouth, and several days after, a good one. Admirably beautiful hands. It was a joy. A joy strong and healthy and true. A shock felt in the entrails as if my strength, worn and weary, had taken on new energy. The consciousness of this being, who will be, this sudden and necessary attachment dominated me entirely. And let us not speak here of sacrifice; this spontaneous devotion born in the heart at this hour is a sustained thing, a law of necessity. You cannot allow life to be extinguished, and everything in the new-born calls for help. Afterwards will come dreams and all the mighty creations of his own charm. The first hour, once again awakens the soul, the first cry cries pity.

Afterwards appeared the whole pageant of resemblances. Was it in him? Was it in me? Is the face of the child a changing mirror where mysterious recollections are reflected and come to life? He recalled to us by turn the uncertain image of St. Vincent de Paul, Talleyrand, an old uncle, my sister who died before him, and his two grandmothers, and his beautiful eyes also recalled those of my father close to his end, as I saw him ill, in this same room where he died.

It is said that a child's first month is without very deep revelations, and that it is not comparable to the surprises which will soon come. Jean's first month brought me a quiet and ever present concern about his breathing. The house in its entirety seemed to me filled with mystery; in the distance as well as close to the silent cradle where he did not cry, we felt the surprising unknown palpitate. The origin of life. And these days were at once anxious, very sweet and almost religious.

◆　◆　◆

Outside in the country, Peyrelebade being a hamlet, so to speak, he had conquered the place, and people approached me to tell me, even before saying good morning, "Is he asleep? How is he?" All the simple, true, good feeling of the peasant who for a long time had never seen a birth inside our walls. The children said to me: "Where is the little sir?" They also came to stand next to the cradle decorated with pink gauze; they stood on their tiptoes to look at him; and they asked me why, like them,

75

he was not tall.

Then the first smile. It came very early, in his sleep, during his second month, on an outing; he was held by his mother seated on a bench; I attracted his eyes by calling him, he looked at me for a long time and smiled at me with tears in his eyes. They won me over.

From this day on, the child, whoever he is, is the anticipation of a poem. Soon, we will read the stanzas of it one by one, and its dominant charm will follow you everywhere. One must have seen births to be able to read this verse of life, so tender, so sensitive, where all graces come together: instinctive love of light, joy in all that moves, taste for movement and curiosity for all that comes before your eyes: trees, vast skies, all sparkling things will speak to him. Jean was always in ecstasy before greenery and his rare tears quickly stopped when he was placed under the chestnut tree in the garden.

And he is no more.

Time does not soften the emotion caused by such a death. It can make one open to activities which fill the hours and make one passionate anew; but in silence at the first hazy leisure, the memory is sensitive and the pain opens the wound.

The death of a child leaves the heart in strife, his memory is always the anticipation of an infinitely sweet feeling which one has tasted and leaves to the unappeased soul a melancholy uneasiness.

To console oneself, one would have to see that there are many others with soft smiles and to love them as much. But the affection of the father is the creation itself of his child: it is his prize, his conquest, his triumph. And this infinite attachment —which is certainty—is a mystery when it is shattered. This proof and revelation have to be imperishable. It seems to me that at the last day, when I go to sleep in the same unknown as he, invisible waves will come close to bring all together, what came from him, what came from me.

◆　◆　◆

1888—People suppose that I have too analytical a mind: it is at least that which comes from the curiosity I feel in the young writers who visit me. I see them the first time they approach me, astonished.

What have I put in my works to suggest to them so many subtleties? I have put in them a little door opening onto a mystery. I have made fictions. It is up to them to go further.

The natural blossoming and growth of a work cannot come from dilettantism. It would serve perfection marvelously if this were possible. It can only happen in small pieces and the author who could achieve the perfect work, would only produce one; he would have touched the absolute and would stop painting.

It is precisely from the regret left by the imperfect work that the next one can be born.

You cannot analyze yourself except after emotion, starting point of all genesis. At the instant one masters one's passion, it is no more. It has served the embryo. All the organs will appear and this requires obedient care, attentive to the germ: the most lucid understanding of his work, at that moment, embryonic but alive; reason, analysis: the intellectual agent will serve the passionate agent and is also brought to life by this latter.

In a word, the nerves of the artist, his sensitivity, his very nature undertake the important business of creation.

◆ ◆ ◆

A thought cannot become a work of art except in literature. Art borrows nothing from philosophy either.

◆ ◆ ◆

All advice shocks us but makes us reflect.

◆ ◆ ◆

To travel is to make contact with certain places that evoke our own life; I felt this in Venice.

                            ◆   ◆   ◆

To Madame Violet—Intelligence is the faculty of understanding. The intelligent man is capable of abstraction, of generalization; he is capable of discovering laws and has no other worries than the pursuit of causes.

The intellectual man, that is to say, termed intellectual, is delighted by the products of the mind and of art, that is, by the moral culture of man. He is a passive and delicate being, alienated from all investigation; he tastes, compares, analyzes, and in not taking sides either for or against, the detachment is itself a pleasure. Intellectuality is a synonym of refinement, distinction, delectation, dilettantism. While the intelligent man, whose most complete incarnation is the scholar, the philosopher, cannot resolve the problem that he undertakes and whose weight crushes him, except in a serious mood tinged by bitterness. His heroism is pitiful; he is the best, his heart is open, he understands a great deal.

The one who takes his eminence only from the spiritual product of others, knows nothing of this sublime uneasiness; he will not move beyond the value of the first one, except if looking at the universal harmony of things, born poet and gifted with a creative sense, he is, then, truly and in a superior manner, the man infinitely complete and necessary who, throughout time and at equal distance from the extremes of evil and good, transmits to other men the supreme element of life, the evocative sediment of joy, the work of art, in a word, the divine fruit.

May 14—The painter is not intellectual when, having painted a nude woman, she leaves in our mind the idea that she will immediately get dressed again. The intellectual painter shows her to us in a nudity that reassures us, because it does not hide her; it leaves her as she is, without shame, in an Eden, for glances that are not ours, but those of a thinking world; an imaginary world created by the painter, where moving and expanding beauty never give rise to indecency but, on the contrary, confer on all nudity a pure charm which does not diminish us. The naked women of Puvis de Chavannes do not put their clothes back on, nor do many others from the past, in the charming women's quarters of a Giorgione or a Correggio.

There is one of them in the *Luncheon on the Grass* by Manet who will hurry to dress herself after the boredom of her discomfort on the cold grass, next to the unidealistic gentlemen who surround her and converse with her. What are they saying? Nothing beautiful I suspect.

As for painting only substances, even very well, with virtuosity, one will taste the pleasure of painting the dress as much as what it is hiding. To paint fabric, fabrics, how much more frank it is and purely decisive, than to represent the nude for the nude, in other words, something of the human being without any heroism.

When Michelangelo affirmed that it was foolish to prefer the shoes of a man to his foot it is because he saw human nature in his very heart, in the vital and active center which swells its lobes, and with which he played to excess to create his style, his great style, of which the ascent is the control of his thought over ours. Under the closed eyes of his slave what elevated intellectual activity! He sleeps, and the anxious dream which unfolds behind this marble brow puts ours in a feeling, thinking world. The sleep of a slave awakens our dignity.

◆　　◆　　◆

March 10, 1889—The admiration of Degas for Ingres is an intellectual love: the heart has nothing to do with it.

Moreover, very conscious, aware of his power, rather than gifted, painting by reflection and combination, not by instinct, his search could lead him to his scholastic idol, this complementary summit of abstract and false art. Starting from the realism of back-stage and the wash-house, to come so far, a curious end which makes one think.

Ingres, however, will never bring life to generous hearts.

But Degas is an artist. He is one, very exultant and free. Coming from Delacroix (of course without his lyricism and his passion!) what a science of juxtaposed tones, exalted, wanted, premeditated, for impressive aims! He is a realist. Perhaps he will be dated by *Nana*. It is naturalism, impressionism, the first stage of the new style. But this proud man will be credited for having all his life held out for liberty. Formerly excluded from an official exhibition by a mistake of the jury, which must have regretted it, he was somewhat avenged. His name, more than his oeuvre, is a synonym of character: it is about him that the principle of independence will always be discussed; and if ever the immeasurable and thick legion which oppresses art, the art of men, would finally recognize the necessity of building within the democratic brood of the average, an annex for the obstinate, the indestructible, Degas would have the right to have his name inscribed high on the temple. Respect here, absolute respect.

◆　◆　◆

April, 1892—*To a journalist from the newspaper "Le Jour".*

The appreciation you have expressed for my works on the occasion of the exhibition of the "Peintres-Graveurs" gives me vivid pleasure. You are the first to state finally that they have, at least, the merit of being made according to the laws of nature herself.

I must confess that this kind of work is inevitably condemned to uneven execution, to groping, because of their diffused source which is in fact an indeterminate ideal; these works could not sustain analysis twice, if they were not fashioned according to the laws of life and of the exterior world.

I believe I have always been a painter, sensorially a painter, particularly in the charcoals and lithographs, and even having shown sometimes a taste for substances. If not, all I have done is worth nothing.

Those who by their writing, or their words, have revealed what is brought to their minds by that which appears mysterious, have caused my astonishment and the surprise of things which had come to me, outside myself, unknown to my willingness. But fortunately you attribute to me, the "tact of values." Thus, those values are for us, so to speak, one of the richest resources of the visible and the most solid support in its realization in our art. In affirming here what you attribute to me, you go straight to the heart of a workman who has long believed he made his dream perceptible by this semblance of the truth.

◆　◆　◆

December, 1897—*Inquiry on Alsace-Lorraine*

I have difficulty answering you. It is difficult for me to speculate on ideas of fighting; I prefer to make only art, and is not art the peaceful refuge, the gentle and high region from which one does not perceive the border? A print by Albrecht Dürer does not incite any revenge, nor does the hearing of the Ninth, nor the affectionate and cordial music of Schumann (to deliberately name the marvels of the lands beyond the Rhine.)

Then, like people of my generation, I have seen the events of 1870 and I have even had the occasion to participate, with much emotion and curiosity in an action on the Loire near Tours: a day of excess, from which I emerged full of pity, troubled, full of the pain of an inexorable hour and as if having endured the abuses of another humanity. And one cannot abstract his reflections; the artist cannot generalize otherwise than through his nerves, and mine shiver, I prefer my dream. War is the great dispute of our misunderstandings.

Then, why guess at a hypothesis? How can we find the reasons for an event that we suppose probable or improbable and tell you in that respect the opinion of others, of the average (which is an abstraction), of young people and of my own? I cannot do it, this really is not my concern. My only hope for joy would be to see a world which would fight no more except to increase its life; which would invade no more except for admiration, or for pity; and whose missiles would be the fruits of the earth, the best and the most sacred, all products human or divine, and also books of art, of thought, of scope, of science, or of good—it is all one.

Peyrelebade, August, 1898—Here we are again under the clear sky of the South, in the same place as in former times, treated with much deference and attention by hosts who left for Vichy, abandoning to us the abandoned house. It is for me like a dream where all my ideas about possession are jostling, and where I feel the most diverse impressions. I could not hide them from you just at this beginning, recalling the attention that you were kind enough to pay to my defeat, and your considering it a benefit for me.

To tell the truth, this big transaction where nothing was sold but an imprint of memories, was also only a little ink put on old papers. What comes of this, however, is the immense and unimaginable lightening of thought that I experienced and that tells me how much reason I was spending here so uselessly. It is impossible that it should not have its repercussion hereafter on my art, which you love; for which I feel an impersonal concern, believe me.

It has been said that what gives the most happiness to man is the sight of things which do not belong to him, like the sea, the mountains, or a great act of heroism. This is obvious: but happiness and production of art do not come from the same alembic and more than ever, I persist in believing that the writer who writes a book in a hotel room is only a dilettante and that the artist who produces truth, human truth, needs, as do other men, to exercise his passion on things, even on those of his own possession. He participates in things that he appropriates and he is not living in abstraction as much as one might believe.

I feel myself completely uprooted.

◆ ◆ ◆

1900—Music is the ferment of a particular sensitivity, very acute, as much as, and even more than, passion itself. It is a danger, a benefit for the person who knows how to take it.

I mean that its charm is irresistible, and one escapes in spirit with it so promptly into a better world, so that sometimes, without deliberation or reasoning, one can postpone the accomplishment of certain tedious acts necessary to us: "Martha, Martha, I have never forgotten you, and I love you more than Mary. It is she who turns me away from you at her hour when she comes. I do not call her."

◆　◆　◆

I love little girls; I see in them all the women, without finding any woman in them, and that is exquisite.

He who would complicate this confession and receive it with a smile will never know what resides in grace. Grace is the revealer of infinite virtuosities and possibilities of life which carry the charm of the spirit through the eyes.

When I was a child, I remember how much I was impressed by them. The first time in the garden of the house where I was born (in Bordeaux, "Allées d'Amour"). She was blonde, with large eyes, and hair in long curls, falling on her muslin dress that grazed me. I felt a shiver, I was twelve, I was going to have my first communion. And chance had it that she was near me during retreats at church, under the mystery of the vaults of Saint-Seurin. How many emotions were involved in it: all the art also of this atmosphere. Blessed hours, will you ever return to the mystery of the unknown?

◆　◆　◆

1901—Oh my soul of former times, soul from afar, you returned to me this evening in the shadows.

Would you agree that I stay with you, in you, to extend those sweet hours?

Friend of night who comes, who goes, that I believe lost forever, what calls you back again and at your hour? I do not know.

◆　◆　◆

1902—The meaning of mystery is to be always in ambiguity, with double, triple aspects; in the hints of aspect (images in images), forms which will be, or which become according to the state of mind of the beholder. All things more than suggestive because they appear.

But this meaning applied to painting requires that the artist have tact, an infinite sense of measure more than for anything else, and the public is not aware of it. It is an art, which, more than any other, demands that an artist be conscious at each moment of its gestation.

From revelations which will not diminish him there is in Delacroix a very acute split between the man and the artist. Whoever has studied his work easily sees in it that he was admirably organized to produce it and to bring it to its achievement. His constancy, his obstinacy, his method, his tenacity to produce, the daily care he took to remain on his guard concerning the masters he loved, his secret and particular studies, in a word, which any creator, whoever he is, pursues unceasingly, he had the law and the formula of it, and the present time is not appropriate to recriminate the form or manner of expression he used. He was himself, from the beginning to the end of his career: this is something that counts, the rest is unimportant.

Moreover, is there not in all true artists a being who is misunderstood by those who are not true artists? The instructive being, forsaken, who recreates himself in his own process, sometimes seems concerned with incomprehensible views: these are not the keys to their genius for those who watch them live; a contemporary, a friend even, can ignore you. Afterwards come new generations, for they who see only the beauty of the result; the work already exists, the process has disappeared, and it is of little importance to us. The life of man is, after all, only the artist's process.

To produce art is not easy; one could call it anti-praiseworthy, unless the artist, to his own detriment, does not cut painfully his life.

He will have to submit to inflexible rules in spending the hours of his time, if he wants to be like common men, and follow the wordly obligations of the society in which he is.

He always acts contrarily, by several strokes that one notices. Those who love him or appreciate him tolerate him nevertheless in his nature, such as he is. In the eyes of others, he differs a little, like the bird of the islands; different demeanor and plumage.

◆　◆　◆

As I complained that nothing was ever given to me, nothing offered, and somebody having remarked that I have during my life neglected many relationships and even friendships, of which some are today powerful in politics and elsewhere. . . . It is because I feel a certain immodesty in expressing a desire. Things should simply fall due, naturally, according to the law of necessity.

A large part of the cake, is on one side of the table; at the other end are the crumbs; well! it should be very easy to sit down at the good side to the satisfaction of all, as if by decency, at this instant when days of lassitude have come to us, when already behind us are accumulated accounts of the effort, of works, and their procession of regrets. Ah! how many wrinkles they have dug into our forehead, and to see them again sometimes with proud surprise nonetheless! Well, it is the moment when without asking for anything, precedence should be given to you in order to enter with the modesty of age and all the vanished charm, into the festive hall. A well-built society should make this possible.

◆　◆　◆

June—The word "social" was very much used during my life. I distrust this word today.

◆　◆　◆

November—I am quite willing to admit that modeling is essential in our art, but on condition that its only aim be beauty. Outside of that this famous modeling is nothingness.

This reflection came to me on viewing a portrait of Waltner by Roybet: the head of a thoughtless man, a life of exasperated sharpness, although without soul. Whoever has seen Waltner at home, letting his imagination run wild, telling you what he thinks about his end, his hopes, his confidence, his great vision of reality which he enlarges up to the boundaries of beyond the grave, his statements on individualism which he denies in order to declare himself a fragmentary being, dependent, branching into the souls of many things. What he thinks and with the sum of generous enthusiasm that his word and his rough face, proud and worthy, exhale, a painter who produces from his head and his eyes only an illusory relief and who makes of his vital brilliance something neutral and animal-like, incapable of turning inward; this portrait painter has done nothing.

Painting is not the representation of the only relief; it is human beauty with the prestige of thought. All that does not incite us to it is null. And the essence of the bad portrait is to not make us feel the presence of the man in the face of the man.

◆　◆　◆

April 12, 1903—The benefits which we ought to receive from our relations with the social world, should not be obtained without having deserved them. Injustice gives to the one who deserves but does not obtain more apparent, even increased superiority. And the person who usurps will always be left with the secret bitterness of envy consuming him. The envious remain envious.

By steadfastness one ends up obtaining.

◆　◆　◆

The work of art is the leavening of an emotion which the artist proposes. The public disposes; but one must love.

◆　◆　◆

June—I cannot say what my sources were. I love nature in all her forms; I love her in the smallest blade of grass, the humble flower, tree, grounds and rocks, up to the majestic peaks of mountains. All things for their own character rather than a whole. I also shiver deeply at the mystery of solitude.

I have loved and I still love the drawings of Leonardo; they are like the essence of life, life expressed by outlines as much as by reliefs. I enjoy their spirit, refined, civilized, aristocratic; I feel in them a serious attraction which lifts me up to high cerebral delectation.

But as to my reading, how to find a link with my art in the pleasure I have in tasting so deliciously the savory writings of our authors, the turn of their thoughts, the rhythm of their style, the breath of their effusion, the spurt, concise or unconstrained, of their mind, their nuances? I do not know. I read abstract things with fatigue, and translations with difficulty and even indifference.

A young and naïve Englishman came to see me once, to tell me that he had crossed the Channel to see me and to learn from me the genesis of my works. "We know their effects," he said, "I would like to be enlightened about their cause." And I learned since, through a friend, who saw him in London, that he returned from his trip extremely disconcerted because I answered him with only a smile. "I could get nothing out of M. Redon," he confessed.

The truth is that one can say nothing about oneself, as to what is born under one's hand, at the thoughtful or passionate hour of gestation. It is often a surprise; you have gone beyond your goal, that is all. What more is there to say! What is the use of analyzing this phenomenon, it would be in vain. Better to renew it for your own joy.

Let us leave the rest to philosophers and scholars.

◆　◆　◆

A landscape of old gold, an engaging softness, a solemn peace, silence, leaves accumulated under your steps. . . .

Oh melancholy perfume of dead leaves which in the gardens, in the autumn, evoke the memory of extinguished lives. . . Sad and funereal charm, under which death would seem sweet, mixed with all that goes away and says to us adieu. . . .

December—Talent is, after all, the acquired power to bring to fruition natural gifts; the notions of experience help us, love of the masters also; I mean those whom we love, not those whom we choose. Certain artists of my time, whom I have seen start out with promise lost themselves for having *chosen* masters whom they ought to love. Their intelligence led them astray in seeking the good and the bad; they have touched the forbidden fruit.

You must love naturally, lazily, for joy, for the joy we will receive one day like a grace. This reveals the necessity of leisure.

Leisure is not a privilege; it is not a favor, it is not a social injustice; it is the beneficial necessity by which the spirit is fashioned as well as taste and the discovery of oneself.

◆ ◆ ◆

A print is an impression on paper, an impression of art unique or multiplied, which requires of the image a human intermediary: the plate leaving all favorable liberty to the sensitivity of the person who prints.

From this, the diversity of proofs, which needs choice, and implies a small number, the rarity.

In former times, the conoisseur recognized the good proof.

◆ ◆ ◆

A portrait is a representation of character, of a human being portrayed in his essence. All the profound life that reveals him on the outside: attitude, expression, moral density.

◆ ◆ ◆

I prefer the spirit of Degas to the spirit of his works.

◆ ◆ ◆

All the humanity in the work of Rodin is not humanity, the beings who flounder and twist there, hysterically, seem to be moved by the electricity of death, the soul absent.

◆　◆　◆

It is not good to take someone into confidence, it would not be understood; at least regarding our genesis. I am told that Carrière who is subtle, however, boasted that he never wanted to paint, and that he remains indifferent to painting itself. He calls himself visionary to the point of being able to extract a human expression from a pebble, not from a face. No painter will admit this; myself least of all.

With respect to this I recall without pleasure that dingy and neutral medium, "terre d'ombre" ("umber"), which he uses and from which emerge his *Maternities*: what he has said invalidates them.

I prefer to proclaim with Pissarro that the art of painting resides, for the one who knows how to look, in a corner of a table, in an apple. To paint an apple, what could be easier! And still to make of this simple notion something which will rise to beauty, it will be necessary that painting be there in its entirety, solid, supple, rich in substance, suggestive almost, of luxury, of grandeur to reveal the presence of man: an atmosphere of thoughts around itself.

And Pissarro has painted the apple alone without all the rest.

◆　◆　◆

Bonnard, a good sort of painter, serving up easel paintings which are often witty! I mean "witty" in the sense of light and smiling.

◆　◆　◆

Painting consists in using a special sense, an innate sense for composing a beautiful substance. To do as nature does: create diamonds, gold, sapphires, agates, precious metal, silk, flesh; it is a gift of delicious sensuality, which can with a bit of simple liquid matter reconstitute or amplify life, imprint a surface from which will emerge a human presence, supreme exposure of the spirit. It is a gift of native sensuality. You cannot acquire it.

◆ ◆ ◆

1906—Limbos . . . opaque limbos where pale faces would float like sea-weed, morbidly human: such is the painting of Carrière. It has not the savour of substances, it stays in the deep regions of a first elaboration favorable to visions and never appears nor flowers in the radiant burst of the solar prism.

He did not know the delectable sensuality of the palette. But on the reduced register of some tempered ochres and brown slate, he has given to sensitive human nature, expressive accents, intimate and pathetic through waving and ephemeral rhythms. He has above all given full flight to his visionary gifts.

Did he have the sense of mystery? I do not see it.

Moreover he came to fruition by the mediocre means—no matter what was said about it—of a public which did not care about it at all, misguided as it was by the tearful and literary song of the maternities that he stupidly made them hear. It would have been good, however, to proclaim that our art has a function entirely different from literature. But what for in the presence of the innumerable and inexorable legion of admirers of Greuze? They are a hydra. An attempt was made to offer them Carrière as prey, with reason perhaps.

Oh time, what will you say? Without you I know that it is color which is the joy of museums. Black cannot be put on the wall except with restraint, in small areas. The error of Carrière was to believe that he could replace the black of charcoal with an oily material.

◆ ◆ ◆

1906—Verbal commentary on Dürer's *Melancholia* by Elémir Bourges:

You see the letter "I" which follows the word Melancolia; this

90

imperceptible sign is the key to it; it means *go* in Latin. And the chimera that takes wing (without being aware of it), carries away the signature of sadness. She goes toward the rising sun, under the liberating rainbow. All the rest is at once explained as being an allegory of science. The tools of work and research are there. This winged being holding a compass, is it not the representation of certainty? Here also is love which inscribes on a tablet an increase of connoisseurship. Leonardo said: "The more one knows, the more one loves."

This commentary puts an end to the suggestive hypothesis and to all verdicts of incoherence. And I smilingly recall having formerly made, just like Dürer, an angel of certitudes; he smiles, a little old man, in a ray of light which dominates a black sky, where I put a questioning glance. I was less aware than Dürer.

This admirable *Melancholia* remains what she always was for me: a rich, deep and ever new source of beautiful abstract lines, which are deep and which reveal amplitude and vastness. I do not know a fuller frame whose structures and planes have so many doors open on the spirit. Tight lines, rich in variety submitted to the serious play of the whole. Without taking pleasure in listening to the music of Bach, I imply here an analogy.

Since my mature age, I always have had this sort of linear fugue before my eyes.

◆　◆　◆

1908—The painter who has found his technique does not interest me. He gets up every morning without passion; calm and peaceful, he continues the work he began the day before. I suspect he feels a certain boredom peculiar to a virtuous worker who continues his task without the unforeseen flash of the happy moment. He has not the sacred torment whose source is in the unconscious and the unknown; he expects nothing of what will come. I love what never has been.

Concern must be the habitual and constant host of the good studio. Concern is like an equation between the palette and the dream. It is the ferment of the new; it renews the creative faculty; it is the witness of sincere mistakes and of the inequality of talent. The man is visible within the artist and the one who looks at his work is then closer to him.

*　◆　◆

July 27, 1909—They are really interesting, a resource of very rich ideas: what an analyst of his own nature! It would be desirable, if he wants to find peace, happiness, that he close his intelligence, his overly conscious clarity (miner's light) in order to concern himself only with the simple substances that he uses.

If he wants to know my experience, it is in what I tell you here; paint, paint; be only in the paint, brushes in hand. Afterwards think of nothing and "smoke your pipe."

As to what he wants to know about the study of the model: all present masters and those of the past have advised, have required the study of nature. But not while "smoking his pipe," no, very actively; on the contrary, with pencil or brush in hand, with for companionship all the reason, all the intelligence of which one is capable.

Bresdin, it is true, never worked from nature; but with him it was inability: I once saw him trying to make a sketch of a horse stopped in front of his window. He started with the ear and finally the head was larger than the entire body. It was the most childish impossibility of giving form to what he saw. But, notice, that for the works with the tiny details that he made, his recollection might have been sufficient. It is quite different with decorative painting which your friend calls "musical painting" and which it would be better to designate: suggestive, moral surface.

Tell him that if he wants to know what is according to me, I mean what I have patiently and slowly acquired, tell him that for this expressive art he is talking about, you must, on the contrary, using his nice expression, "examine with near-sightedness the blade of grass or the pebble."

It is after having said this sort of rosary that imagination will take flight and with her all the effervescence and all the exaltation necessary. Beyond the resource of keeping documents in boxes (still alive and instructive), even when the paper they are on has yellowed. It happens thus when minutely, patiently, obstinately, you have arranged all the folds of your life, there is a sort of imaginative power ready to burst forth; it is in itself the source of this suggestive art.

I am speaking here only about myself; but I confess sincerely: I had to go through studies which are, in a certain way, the contrary of the stained glass window your friend has seen. The painter must have with him, under his hand, *fixed elements*. I don't think you can avoid this. No visual memory will be able to supply it.

I know that the earth turns, that all passes away, and even that it is necessary, Renan said, for the gods to change, but I am unable at the instant when I breathe and write to you to think about my art differently: eat the *bait* by the most attentive, the most meticulous analysis, pencil in hand: that is my system.

I failed this rule in the hours of sin. But repentance is a new innocence when it is followed by rehabilitation through restorative action. Action that would not come without sin (in other words, experience; in other words, knowledge). And please believe me that gentle and light is the serenity which flows from this understanding of oneself!

Your friend should not try to find himself through formulas, or doctrines; he should work: the oracle will speak to him as if by surprise at the instant when he has the brush in his hand. Not when he reflects.

Less analysis, except of the materials he uses and which attract him. They, too, carry within themselves a part of the secret. They are better advisors than masters. They surpass all theories. He should subtly examine their resources. The more he knows them, the more his spirit will illuminate them. The fullness of expressive art irradiates only through substances. Your friend is not without a presentiment of this.

◆ ◆ ◆

1909—Art borrows nothing from philosophy and has no other source than the soul in the midst of the world surrounding it. Its essence is unknown, as is the essence of life; and its goal is art itself. Maurice Denis weighs his art down with social and religious assignments; he touches upon politics, which is a pity. His gifts were capable of placing him in a better position, higher than in a blind alley. His honesty will keep him from any narrow-mindedness.

◆　◆　◆

To submit talent and even genius to concepts of justice or morality is a great error. With the artist, it proceeds from predominance of speculative intelligence over free divination.

◆　◆　◆

A work conceived for the purpose of teaching will be led along wrong paths. A picture teaches nothing; it attracts, it surprises, it exalts, it leads imperceptibly and by love to the need for living with beauty; it raises and refreshes the spirit, that is all.

◆　◆　◆

No, you must not put your art in the chains of political convictions or of morality. On the contrary, art should provide the philosopher, the thinker, the scholar and perhaps even the theosophist—who knows?—with themes for speculation and for love.

◆　◆　◆

The mysterious origin of a vocation is irreducible, like love, like death.

◆　◆　◆

May, 1910—What a strange investigation: they speak of bringing the remains of Puvis de Chavannes to the Panthéon.

But having seen in previous times the laughing and amused crowd which pressed before his paintings, notably *The Poor Fisherman* and *Hope*, I cannot entertain the idea except with a sad smile.

Does not this sudden change of favor show the eternal and fluctuating caprice of human recognition? To tell the truth, those who were indifferent, still are, and the opposed demonstration of today probably hides from us many uncertain things.

I do not subscribe to this wish, as the transfer of the mortal remains of famous and unknown people painfully touches my sensitivity, and even my thought. On the contrary, I see a certain grandeur in respect for the place, humble or sumptuous, where parents and friends have cried before the beloved, laid down there at the supreme and heartbreaking hour of death. This place remains a fatal sign, not measured by our standards nor by our justice. It is of another order.

That cannot be helped.

That which does not change, that which is forever alive and present is the permanent action of a master through the works he has left. Puvis de Chavannes has an ever active voice in the Panthéon, in the frescos of Sainte-Geneviève. Why add to them the ashes whose silence, after all, belongs to the unknown?

The glorification and apotheosis of a great man are in the honor we pay him by giving a visible and high place to his works during his lifetime or after it.

It would be interesting to see in Parliament a concern for taking care of art differently than for a collectivity. What? An artist or a poet would be taken care of there! The great muralist Puvis de Chavannes is worth the trouble; he was worth the trouble.

◆　◆　◆

July—*For a note in a catalogue.*

I do not address the metaphysical spirits here, neither do I address the pedagogues because they do not have their eyes fixed on the beauties of nature; their menial habits keep them too far from the intermediary ideas which link sensations with thoughts: their minds are too occupied with abstractions to fully share and taste the delights of art, which always suppose the connection between the soul and real, exterior objects.

I address those who surrender docilely, without the help of sterile explanations to the secret and mysterious laws of sensitivity and of the heart.

From day to day, the artist submits to the fatal rhythm of the impulses of the universal world which envelops him. Continuous center of sensations, ever flexible, hypnotized by the marvels of the nature that he loves, he scrutinizes; his eyes, like his soul, are in constant touch with the most fortuitous phenomena. He leans toward that communion which is sweet to him when he is a painter. How could he leave a state in which he delights and restrains himself to enter, like the scholar or the esthete, into generalization? He cannot: this action outside of himself is impossible to him. Do not ask him to be a prophet; he gives only his fruit, that is his function.

If, by some arduous operation, which is difficult, very difficult, he compares himself to others in order to judge them, he will have to remove his eyeglasses to see with clarity, without any help, the fruit of others. He will know how to speak well only of himself, of his adventure, of the unique circumstance, happy or tragic, where his destiny placed him.

As for me, I believe I have made an art that is expressive, suggestive, undetermined. An art that suggests is the irradiation of divine plastic elements brought together, combined in order to call forth dreams that it illuminates, exalts and incites to thought.

If my art did not initially find an echo in the public of my rationalist generation, where an edifice with the rather low arches of Impressionism has been built, the present generation (as everything evolves) understands it better. Youth, though, has quite a different mentality, touched more than in former times in France by the supreme waves of music, necessarily open also to fictions and to dreams of the idealistic form of this art.

◆　◆　◆

On the loss of his property in Peyrelebade
We are held to certain places by invisible attachments which are like organs for the creative man.

Perhaps it is in the submission to things by an act of will, of liberty, of tact, of docility, to the necessities of the unconscious, that we find originality. It is said that Beethoven needed to return to a house that he had left; he needed it to complete a symphony. Who could believe it for music, however, that art of interior life. I understand it. To leave an accustomed place has always been a kind of death for me. Life returns elsewhere afterwards, but differently, and one fears this unknown. I cannot tell you the profound torment a simple move, a change of home, gives me. I am stagnant. In order to return to life and a taste for work in the new dwelling where I will be, I need time, much time, even seasons. All this will tell you what it meant to me to break away from the old house at Peyrelebade, where what I have done with the most intensity, passion, and spontaneity surged before my eyes: all the surprises of myself, all my consciousness as an artist, beside the memories.

To leave a familiar place is like dying. From this comes the terror of a new beginning elsewhere. In fact, I owe to my country those sad faces that you know and that I drew because I saw them and because the eyes of my childhood had preserved them for the intimate resonances of my soul. Yes, an old bare wall, an old tree, a certain horizon, can be the nourishment and vital element of an artist; there where he has rooted. The day when Rembrandt advised his students against traveling and above all to Italy; I think he was the forerunner of profound art.

Art is, for one who loves it, a pillar; you cannot deny the support you find there for spiritual maintenance. The reading of a beautiful book, of a single page of this book, the accent of a chord of supreme harmony, a known song heard suddenly, acts on us, seizes us, holds us unexpectedly in a pensive state.

I thought in former days that art was useless: it might perhaps be necessary.

◆　　◆　　◆

September, 1911—Mona Lisa is consecrated, I mean by this that she has received, in the flow of time over four centuries, the homage of being admired by masters. It was not for her smile; but if painting in its essential strictness has as a goal to produce on a flat surface, through the play of light and dark, the greatest possible relief of one of the elements of nature, even if only a human face radiant with spirit, this aim is attained by Leonardo, at its full height, its full strength, indeed to a prodigious degree.

December—*To Monsieur X . . .*

Would you be so kind as to tell me what you mean by the word *Humanist* that you use in an appreciation of my works on the occasion of a recent exhibition.

While thanking you for your expression of praise, which touches me, as it is obvious that you like my work, I confess that I understand nothing about the word "humanism" placed there.

To enlighten you more about my inquiry, let me tell you what is in my thoughts: a well born artist must at the close of his career make a kind of self-examination where he reviews and sees if he has used to a good end the natural gifts he has received. I am beyond a half century at this hour, and that is sweet and delightful to me. I declare it often to young artists, to make clear to them what good they will find in old age, if they have the wisdom and the honesty to remain always themselves; in other words, to cultivate the flower of their own garden, a unique flower, humble or luxurious, but which will always be the mark of their mastery.

I think I have offered, in the past more than now, in drawings and lithographs. varied and human expressions; I have even, by permissible fantasy, placed them in a world of unlikelihood, in imaginary beings that I have tried to make logical with the logic of the structure of visible beings. But I feel certain that in their regard this word humanism cannot be applied at all.

What does it express then under your pen?

I mean this humanism in connection with a work of art. You can explain it to me in a few lines.

(This letter never received a reply.)

◆   ◆   ◆

How sweet it would be to age if the stream of years dried up in us the source of pain! But no. On the slope on which we are descending, we have a too faithful companion: the heart does not leave us.

It describes with us an inverse spiral—it approaches an ever blacker point which is the end, the irresistible end.

What can the insatiable do there?

◆　◆　◆

1912—You have only to stuff your ears in a concert hall to think you are in an insane asylum. With one sense less, you are attending an incomprehensible phantasmagoria.

In art, seemingly, the man of genius, whoever he may be, with a sixth, seventh sense dances before the deaf, talks to the dumb, paints for the blind; and the result he obtains is absurd.

This should console the artist in his strange and fatal condition, of appearing in the midst of others; only to produce a burst of laughter.

He carries the folly which will win out; it is the advent of a new sense which will come to those who look at him and deny him: a growth of life even for those who are not yet aware of it.

"Flowers, almost theoretical, subjecting the visual aspect to the overall impression which has captured thought." This may be true except for the idea of theory.

Anyway, this appreciation controls and determines some of my works. It is possible that halfway toward realization a sudden aid to my memory sometimes forced me to stop certain works for the result mentioned here, finding them formed and organized according to my wish: flowers at the confluence of two river banks, that of representation and that of memory. It is the soil of art itself, the good earth of the real, harrowed and tilled by the spirit.

I have often, as an exercise and as sustenance, painted before an object down to the smallest accidents of its visual appearance; but the day left me sad and with an unsatiated thirst. The next day I let the other source run, that of imagination, through the recollection of the forms and I was then reassured and appeased.

Art criticism is not creative.

You can accept it from thoughtful and sensitive people who are able to be especially objective; people gifted with communicative and fervent joy which will reflect through love and admiration something of the beauty they cherish: a flame bursting from the divine hearth which gains in breadth and gives birth to other flames.

But commentary, pure commentary, is excusable only when it incessantly remolds principles, ever anew, at each thrill of a new art. It must proclaim discoveries.

◆　◆　◆

An inquiry into the lives of painters? What for? Can one believe that he will find revelations there that will bring justice to them? What's the use?

The artist comes to life for a fulfillment which is mysterious. He is an accident. Nothing awaits him in the social world. He is born naked on the straw, without a mother having prepared his swaddling clothes. As soon as he offers, young or old, the rare flower of originality—which is and ought to be a unique flower—the perfume of that unknown flower will disturb heads and everybody will turn aside. From this, for the artist a fatal, even tragic isolation, from this, the irremediable and sad disquietude which envelopes his youth and even his childhood and which makes him fierce sometimes until the day when he finds, by affinity, beings who will understand him.

It would be better not to speak about those painful origins: to know them will change nothing. Something from destiny or necessity assigns to each his way, along which we encounter difficulties, large or small, as does everyone. It is not justice which matters to us, it is love. What matters the most is to know that our works are recognized, appreciated, desired.

As for me, I usually turn my thoughts away from my painful genesis. Too weak for the struggle or maybe disdaining it, I waited; I put out, as I could and when circumstances permitted, works which were loved by a small circle around me. I believe they pleaded my cause far and away much better than I could have done it myself. It is they who cleared a way for me and who tell

100

my story. I have good reason to believe that the most recent will speak of the joy that compensates for the bad beginning.

◆ ◆ ◆

April, 1913—*On Jean Dolent*

Let us remember that he wrote this: "To live without noise is a consolation for living without glory." Why should we not be consoled, we, too, by remaining faithful to him, reading him and loving him in silence? We would be there in his thoughts, and silence is not forgetfulness. Whoever painted formerly, in the preceeding generations, whoever paints today will always remember his writings and the splendid independence he showed in the defense of the independent masters. I pay homage to Jean Dolent because he loved painters, and all those who by their attitude and character have cared about art, uniquely art for art's sake, for art only. These are not legion, they are rare. They go their way resigned to live without noise, producing work that has no alloy. No politics, no social views.

The others? Ah! how he has teased and shaded them with his delicious mockery! Their work and their talk activated and fertilized his prankish spirit. Your inquiry put back into my hands his books of light reading, written in a cursive and rapid style, a style that is not apparent and leaves us at ease without the influence of literature (which is good in the discipline of a painter). His strokes are like strokes of etchings, and they contain double, even triple meanings, as was his talk.

I could not tell you how enjoyable and good is the memory I have of him. To meet him was pleasant. We came together by attraction; as if by a previous agreement, derived from surrounding things we knew without speaking about, and our comments about them, in view of his age and mine, were expressed between us by a smile.

He is one of those about whom I regret that the complications of life and work did not allow me to see more often.

◆ ◆ ◆

101

I see in a window a book with the title *Social Art*. It is disgusting. I open it nevertheless, and I see: Socialization of beauty, and I close it.

◆　◆　◆

You can learn only from yourself: it is difficult to teach. All the masters have advised studying nature and agree on this subject; but they differed in the means given to do so, because they were all different.

◆　◆　◆

January, 1913—*For a lecture given in Holland on the occasion of an exhibition of his works*

These are not memories I recount, but opinions about me, confessions, testimony for the sole purpose of indirectly shedding light on my art. I owe it this. In spite of knowing its defects and weaknesses, I have respect for it. I recalled its significance and the extent of its grasp on the spirit, of some echoes so touching, so sincere, unexpected, even awakening my surprise, that I do nothing but participate in its expansion, still attending to it with a pen, and trying to project into the minds of some others a little farther away, something again of its initial effect.

And rest assured that I write here dispassionately, without haughtiness, with nothing of myself, but with the wish to subtract from it. I would not like to give up either reserve, or discretion, which it is decent to keep when talking about an art that is yours. All is not vanity for one who accepts his gifts with grateful curiosity, with no envy toward the gifts of others: he submits peacefully to the care of cultivating his faculties for the pleasure of gathering their fruition and of sharing them with those who wait for them and love them. I therefore continue the flow of this narration for them, for those who will approve my task, and who will be able to see how simple it is.

Formerly, when I produced drawings and lithographs and published them, I often received letters from strangers telling me of their attachment to this art, and revealing to me an exalted emotion. One of them confessed to having been touched to the point of religious feeling and having received faith from them. I do not know if art has such power; but since then, I have had to face with more consideration certain of my works, particularly those executed in hours of sadness, of pain, and which for this very reason, are probably more expressive. Sadness, when it is without cause, is perhaps a secret fervor, a sort of oration, something vaguely like worship, in the unknown.

Consequently, I looked at and scrutinized my blacks and it is above all in the lithographs that those blacks have their integral brilliance, unalloyed, for the charcoal drawings which I made before them and since, were always made on paper tinted with pink or yellow, sometimes blue, thus showing my tendency or premise for color in which I later found the utmost pleasure and which overwhelmed me with delight.

Black is the most essential color. It takes above all its exaltation and life—shall I confess it?—in the deepest and most discreet sources of health. The secret, vital ardor that gives birth to charcoals depends on good diet and rest, or better, let us say, on the plenitude of physical strength. That is to say, it will appear in its full and greatest beauty at the very heart of our career, whether short or long. It is exhausting later in old age when nourishment is less assimilated. At that point one can always spread black matter on a surface, but charcoal stays carbon, the lithographic crayon transmits nothing; in a word, the matter remains in our eye such as it appears, an inert and lifeless thing; whereas at the happy hour of effervescence and propitious strength, from the matter springs the very vitality of a being, his energy, his spirit, something of his soul, mirror of his sensitivity, residue of his substance, in a way.

Black should be respected. Nothing prostitutes it. It does not please the eye and does not awaken sensuality. It is the agent of the spirit much more than the splendid color of the palette or of the prism. Therefore, the good print will be enjoyed more in a somber country where harsh nature constrains man to be confined at home, cultivating his thought, as in the regions of the North, for example, and not as in those of the South, where the sun draws us outdoors and enchants us. It is not highly regarded in France, except as impoverished by color, giving a different result, which annihilates the print and brings it close to the image.

Pencil is hardly more appreciated. There is at the Louvre in the drawing galleries a quantity of art much larger and purer than in the painting galleries; one seldom goes there, preferring to visit the paintings. It is because the pleasure for the eye is here. This is a clear indication of the similar indifference which in France will always greet the work of the artist who delights in the austerity of black. Thus, I watched the attempts at publishing my catalogues there without believing too much in the possibility, I confess.

At that time, they were to appear on the Boulevards. Could one imagine an alert and amused passerby on these boisterous walks seriously taken by a publication of this sort? No; these strange lithographs, often dark, abstruse, and let us say, with hardly a seductive appearance, call forth, on the contrary, the spirits of silence and some of them even rare resources of natural ingenuity, a kind of grace.

To tell all my thoughts, I have always believed that my public was far from these parts, as was proven by the first attention given to me: it was at first beyond the borders of my country that my works were in demand and loved.

What a good public is the one that has never seen anything! The dilettante, when without love, maintains in himself a disastrous defect: the need for analysis and the accumulation in his memory of all he has seen (a considerable accumulation, and always amplified in our time). This mental impediment turns him away from fresh and fertile naïveté; his sensitivity is no longer free; he does not give in to it, at least in Paris, but in the acute tension of not being the dupe of an impression, which he always wants to be lucid and then intellectual, of which he will speak at once, as is fitting, usually with a light vivacity, and even a smile. The seriousness of the character of art, on the contrary, acts on beings whose attention and disposition are thoughtful. The same is true for the one who creates it: the artist knows perfectly that among all of his works the one which reflects and reveals him the most was done in solitude. All genesis retains a little shadow and mystery. It is in solitude that the artist feels himself intensely alive, in secret depth, and nothing of the outside world solicits him nor obliges him to disguise himself. It is there that he feels, discovers that he sees, finds, desires, loves and saturates himself with the natural, at the primary sources of instinct, it is there, more than in any other social place, that he is given the power to become exalted with purity and to illuminate by his spirit the raw material he opens and spreads.

My first lithographs, published in 1879, were mostly repetitions or variations of drawings I had made long before, for myself alone, in the full isolation of the country. The view of the peaceful work of the fields was the only diversion which could distract me from them. Nothing is as propitious for the production of art as a flow of distractions in opposition to the art itself: the same as light physical occupation which puts into the brain a certain productive effervescence. How many times, oh sincere witness, have I not taken the charcoal with a hand made brown by the earth, that I had just touched while gardening! Sacred and silent material, restorative source and refuge, how indebted am I to you for gentle appeasements! What balm has ever had on me, on my spririt, and even on my sorrows, a more sudden action, more salutary than the view of green grass or the contact with any other unconscious element. Leaving the city, going to the fields, approaching a village in its rustic quietness; it is there, always, that I have felt the tremors of my beating heart which have made me solemn, and which in a sudden communion with myself, I stammered, distracted, that the truth of life was to live there—perhaps.

But it is vain to recriminate what was not, could not be. And the past, moreover, does it not leave to the present a margin on which the future can inscribe better days? And is not here, also, the consoling benefit of old age, this inexorable but also lucid time when one can more easily be wise in the new light offered by the good advice of memory?

One makes his talent evolve and progress in the same way.

The artist who creates with a concern for perfection, I mean the concern to offer with candor a work autonomously gratifying, a work in which will be revealed his unique personality; this one will always put his name on his work with reluctance, or with some constraint. And it is this strife, this uneasiness of conscience which is the fatal element of the next new beginning, the ferment of the next work, with the aim to do it better.

Thus I kept a watch over myself through my creations. Oh! without pride, looking at myself carefully, a little as a scholar would look at the appreciable phenomena of nature's functioning to acquire broader experience. And I discerned the sudden influence exerted on me by different places or times, seasons, my home, the orientation of the light in the studio, so that I assert here with certainty and confidence how much we must reckon with the invisible moving, palpable world that surrounds us and makes us bend under the still mysterious and unexplained pressures of the outside.

Every fold made in us, in a particular place, becomes modified, unknown to us, in another. I think that the great style of Rembrandt, this style born from the heart and from a spirit capable of wide expansion is caused by the stagnation of his quiet life. He never left Amsterdam and never advised his students to make journeys, even to Italy. And without wanting to say here that immobility provides genius, I believe that his humble and sublime vision would have gained nothing by the multiplication and accumulation of sensations gathered far from the constant models he had before his eyes. He might have lost in diversity what he kept in himself, unique and deep in the solitary refuge of his dreams and of his thoughts. And see also how at the end of his life, as much as in his worldly and glorious years with Saskia, he gives full flight to the play of his best fibre, to compassion. It is certain, then, that he frequents people who do not belong to the world, but to the street, to the modest districts of the poor, where he is, where he lives, where the deepest energies of the soul and of the instinct grumble and flutter and become exasperated.

Besides the dispositions received under the influence of the world and the place that surrounds him, the artist also submits, in a certain way, to the exacting requirements of the material he uses: pencil, charcoal, pastel, oily paste, engraving ink, marble, bronze, clay or wood—all these products are agents that accompany him, collaborate with him, and also have something to tell in the fiction he will accomplish. The material reveals secrets, it has its genius; it is through it that the oracle will speak. When the painter offers something of his dream, do not forget the action of those secret traces which bind him and tie him to the ground with a lucid and well awakened spirit, quite the contrary.

The greasy lithograph crayon operates indirectly: it is the intermediary which transmits and multiplies the work; and the sensitivity of the artist must reckon also (alas) with the inevitable promiscuity of the printer. The precious fruit of the artist's spirit is entrusted to him, there is no choice; but nothing good, nothing accomplished will be possible without the careful collaboration of this assistant, simple craftsman whose participation is precious when it is intuitive, disastrous and deplorable when he does not feel or guess anything. You make a temporary, badly matched union with him and by reason you have to come into agreement with him. But a work of art cannot be born from a team of two. One of them must yield.

My God, how I have suffered with printers, how I have experienced within myself bursts of rage at the statements of confused incomprehension issuing from the printer of my trial proofs. I knew those proofs were unevenly shaped, outside of the methods usually followed for working on stone: but I was searching, I have searched. And I believe I have used my imagination with abandon and without restraint for exacting from the resources of lithography all that it could give. All my prints, from the first to the last, were nothing but the fruit of curious, attentive, anxious, and passioned analysis; of what power of expression could be contained in a greasy lithograph crayon, with the aid of paper and stone. I am astonished that artists have not further expanded this simple and rich art, obeying the most subtle impulses of sensitivity. The time in which I lived must have been quite preoccupied with direct imitations and naturalism for this process, not to have captivated the inventive spirits of fictions and attempted to lead them to deploy the suggestive richness that it contains. It challenges and makes the unexpected appear.

I speak here about the paper, the so called "tracing paper," much more than about the stone. The stone is harsh, unpleasant, like a person who has whims and fits. It is impressionable, and submits to the most moving and variable influences of the weather. If it rains, if it snows, if the temperature is hot or cold, as many conditions, deceptive or happy, fertile with pleasant or unpleasant surprises, and dictating the attitude you must have with it, when you print. Thus, next to it the daily routine of life is unbearable. It is better to forsake it deliberately, forget it, it and its texture as one neglects, alas, by the force of circumstances and in spite of all virtue, certain old-fashioned and respectable people with whom you are bored, because the life and interest one brings to present things are no more in them.

The future of lithography (if it has one) lies in the resources, still to be discovered, of paper, which transmits so perfectly to the stone the finest and moving inflections of the spirit. The stone will become passive.

These reflections awaken the remembrance of Rodolphe Bresdin, who initiated me, with the greatest concern for my independence, into the art of etching and lithography. He did not practice it on paper; he did not use a crayon either. This visionary, whose eyes and heart were openly fixed on the visible world, stippled with the pen alone the most minute elements proper to the expression of his dream. He left, besides, some wonderful etchings, several stones where the composition of the blacks is solid. He shaped them with the constant anxiety that this ink gave him. He diluted it seriously, peacefully, preciously; and one felt, looking at him, how much this initial procedure, so indifferent to others, was decisive for him, in a certain way. He took great consideration and care with this liquid; he kept away all dust, whose disastrous presence might become an obstacle to the final result of the work. He reminded me then, with his minute cares, of that Dutch master who, with a precautionary sense similar to his, had placed his working studio in a cellar where no one but he could go, where he descended slowly and softly in order not to raise a single injurious atom which could disturb the purity of his oils and his colors.

Bresdin, although born French near the Loire, had in his taste and life something of the masters of great substance. He was poor and had about him precarious things, but everything his fine hands touched brought to mind the idea of a rare and precious object. When he worked, his tapered fingers looked as if lengthened by fluids which tied them to his tools. These were not the hands of a priest, as we say, these were conscious hands, loving, sensitive to substances, not disdainful of humble objects, but still refined, elegant, soft and supple, like those of the aristocracy. The hands of an artist. They clearly revealed, like his entire person, a being quite apart, and of a fatal destination, a being predestined to suffer secretly, painfully, the daily blows of ordinary life, against the life of his pure and tender love. The artist, this accident, this being for whom the social world holds nothing, except for the love and admiration of a few, of random relationships, the artist, born without fortune, is condemned, to submit to all the hardships of disenchantment. But Bresdin, by a natural gift of playfulness and joy, nobly bore the wounds of destiny: to those who were able to see, his outward appearance expressed goodness.

He was of medium height, stocky and powerful, with short arms. A face with clear and fine eyes. A calm, high forehead which not a single wrinkle had furrowed.

He gardened willingly, and with the minute precision of a Chinese. Subtle in everything and meticulous, he brought to it his finesse, his delicacy, his curiosity of analysis and observation. It was then more than at any other moment that his spirit was alert and that he overflowed in spurts of sudden and impressive words which left me pensive. Once he told me with gentle authority: "Look at this chimney flue. What does it say to you? To me it tells a legend. If you have the strength to observe it well and to understand it, imagine the most strange, the most bizarre subject; if it is based and remains within the limits of this simple section of wall, your dream will be alive. Art is there." Bresdin told me this in 1864. I note the date because it was not the manner of teaching at that time.

I declare myself happy today having heard, as a youth, from an original and total artist whom I loved and admired, these non-subversive words which I understood so well and which confirmed me in my own presentiment. They give in an apparently simple form, the preliminaries of the highest teaching. They open the eyes of the painter on the two worlds of life, on two realities impossible to separate, without diminishing our art and depriving it of what it can provide that is noble and supreme.

The artists of my generation for the most part have surely looked at the chimney flue. And they saw nothing but it. They have not offered all that could be added to the wall panel through the mirage of our very nature. All that surpasses, illuminates or amplifies the object and elevates the mind into the realm of mystery, to the confusion of the irresolute and of its delicious restlessness, has been totally closed to them. They kept away, they feared everything pertaining to the symbolic, all that our art contains of the unexpected, the imprecise, the undefinable, and that gives it an appearance bordering on enigma. True parasites of the object, they cultivated art on a uniquely visual field, and in a certain way, closed it off from that which goes beyond it, and which might bring the light of spirituality into the most modest trials, even in the blacks. I mean an illumination that seizes our spirit and escapes all analysis.

On the evidence of those gaps which cannot be denied, one might feel regret if one lost the recollection of all that was blooming everywhere in my youth. Those who, like me, have seen the course of the production of that epoch will understand how much the artists with closed minds, of whom I speak, had their reason for being, alas, and how much they obeyed, consciously or not, a law of necessary rejuvenation and refreshment. All the development of the influence of David, by his students and their pupils, was officially in full swing: captive production, dry, devoid of exuberance, issue of an abstract formula, when it was only necessary to open their eyes naively on the magnificence of nature to liberate and revive this production.

All things considered, we should, even so, be thankful to those of my contemporaries who have followed the right path, the path of truth in the forest of high trees. If the trees there are not of full height, if the sky there is a little low and the clouds too heavy to entrust to them our dreams, some of those artists have still walked there resolutely and vigorously, with the swagger of convinced rebels who hold for an instant a part of the truth within the truth. If the structure they have built does not have deep perspectives, at least the air there is pure, and one can breathe.

Bresdin did not know their struggles, because he belonged to another time: he came into being in 1822. And the little village where he was born set before his eyes in his childhood only peaceful, rustic scenes of the countryside. He did not dream of making them better, he loved them. All urchin, already, he scribbled and engraved on copper and the vicar of the village, surprised by his attempts, was, he told me, his first patron. Oh! the good vicar who added to the austere practice of his ministry a little concern for art. Tolerating some emancipation, as well, he enlightened Bresdin's parents on the vocation of the child and advised them to let him leave, to pursue elsewhere, in a better environment, another future than the one they were preparing for him. His father was a tanner.

In what region, in what social world could have arisen in this child such a precious disposition which later gave birth to the rare flower of originality! It is presumed that later on, when Bresdin carved the touching images of the *Flight to Egypt*, this subject that he loved and varied so often, it is presumed that he thought of the good vicar who had shown him the divine star. He did nothing but travel, always in imagination, toward better worlds. He drew families traveling, barbarians emigrating, armies, legions or populations in flight. I don't know how to emphasize the richness and variety of his works, which nobody knows because the proofs are rare and scarce.

He told me his mother was of the nobility—I think I remember this—and this origin might explain the dissimilar traits of character one could perceive in him. He was both commoner and aristocrat. He probably owed to this descent the pecularities of his strange nature, fantastic, childish, blunt and good, suddenly retiring within himself, suddenly open and playful. The naturalness of his talks gave good advice received without the weariness which usually goes with solemn teaching. With him everything was light and led you to meditate, often even with a smile. It was true humor. He did not understand

and did not like academic art. He was shocked that a certain master talked about "honesty" in connection with drawing. "Color is life itself," he used to say. "It abolishes line under its radiance." And one felt that his convictions on this point belonged only to himself and to the veneration he had for natural and instinctive invention.

Alas! how much that I heard from him was different from what was heard in the schools! What teaching have we received? and even those who have followed me? Is it possible, during the teacher's rounds through the studio among the students in front of the model, to give each one the right word, the fertile word, the one that will seed each brow according to its particular law? No, not easily. In every student, in each child, is there not the extraordinary mystery of what he will be? And will the teacher have the touch that is sufficiently gentle, the insight that is sufficiently fine and prophetic to put into fruitful flowering the first stammerings of his student?

One who teaches, after all, wishes nothing better than to continue the work of the masters, but alas, even only to transmit it, he does not quite have their permission. Indeed he indulges in them as he is able, as best he can, as does the grammarian by analysis of the beautiful works of the past which time has consecrated, but there he acquires only abstract experience, all in formulas, where the engaging authority of love is missing. One must love in order to believe, one must believe in order to act: the best teaching, then, will be received from one who already has touched the apprentice through a sort of creative revelation that issues from the beauty of his own works.

It is no longer like this today. My friend Stéphane Mallarmé, always moved by the spirit of magnificent independence, desired the abolition of the lycée as much as of the guillotine.

Perhaps he was thinking about the requirements of his life as a teacher, but he also thought, no doubt, about the rather insufficient teaching the student receives and simultaneously shares with an entire group of his fellows. It is far more difficult for him to find himself there than when he is alone, without constraint.

To speak here only about the painting student at the Academy, I would compare him with the seed that the sower has thrown onto the field to bring it to fertilization randomly by the plough that passes blindly over it, haphazardly heaping over it earth that will or will not be helpful.

The plough is the rule, the lycée, the academy of painting, the indifferent teacher, perhaps without love, who comes on a fixed day and hour because it is his job. The student is here far away from the gentle and beneficial leisure and the blessed hours where intuition will guide him.

I believe in teaching what is fruitful by natural communication, with a teacher of our own choice and even in intimacy if possible, such as it was practiced in former times.

Near Bresdin nobody forgot either the veneration for nature or for the masters, particularly for Rembrandt whom he adored. "Rembrandt," he used to say, "painted nothing but beggars, crippled, gouty, and still what nobility, what loftiness, what poetry, what divinity: he has something of God!"

I liked to give this fervent disciple something of the master he venerated. Just like him, he lived in a humble suburb where his bearing and his gait inspired some suspicion in the poor who surrounded him: it was noticeable. He was mysterious himself. He was that way, not by contempt, but by a natural superiority and so as to keep pure and more active the interior resources of his own life. People do not understand this kind of relationship. They can only admit them in a range of actions other than those of an artist whose pain they cannot even imagine. They are unaware of the bruising which the refinement of culture encounters in promiscuity. But the artist, nevertheless, without mixing with the people, will always be fond of their spontaneity because it nourishes his vision of the natural, and, more than in worldly places, he finds there native generosity of gesture and passions.

I saw him in Bordeaux, in extreme distress, which he forgot in frantic labor. His street, with an ancient name, no longer bears the name of "Fosse-aux-Lions"[1] to which he called my attention for fun with a smile. It was next to the beautiful cemetery of the Chartreuse, which I used to cross sometimes when going to see him in the first hours of the morning. It was in the spring. This season in Bordeaux has delicious softness; the air there is

---

[1] Lion's Den

113

humid and warm under a clear sky, the light is limpid. I don't know if it is the retreat of time that thus magnifies the impressions of youth, but nowhere and never have I felt so strongly the refreshing agility of my walks all along the solitary lanes on narrow sidewalks which led me to him. Those were half-built areas without human agglomeration, where trees emerged from gardens over the low walls or hedgerows, where hawthorn flowers fallen on the sidewalks, and which I trampled under foot, plunged me into strange reveries.

At this moment of the year and, moreover, of our youth, with what freshness sensitive fibres vibrate in us! And how much do motives change: I would not walk over flowers today. It would seem to me like committing a desecration; it would seem to me rude to mutilate them, although fallen and their brief life already ended, those fragile perfumed beings, exquisite prodigies of light. In former times I crushed them with sensual pleasure for the strange shiver I felt, and the even stranger stream taken by my thoughts when doing that. It was like an obscure remembrance of things prior to my own days, the echo of soft joys, of happy enchantments. And this was in contrast to my usual state of mind, at that time so morose and melancholy. In the same notebooks where I keep the words of my old friend Bresdin, which I noted in secret, as I also hid from him my own, I find these lines written in sickly handwriting, which I give you, like the premises of my blacks, of my shadows—and that I would no longer write today: "I walked along the cold and silent paths of the cemetery and near the deserted tombs. And I have known the calm of the spirit. Oh death how broad you are: in the calm given to me by the thought of you, what strength against sorrow!"

I do not wish to transcribe anymore: simple indication of a state of spirit which often came under my pencils. But time, time in which we incessantly unfurl our accomplishments, offered me, as it did to all human beings, a more vivid light. And those first sorrows, felt far beyond my youth itself, have had to vanish in the truer accord between my strengths and my desires. By continuously objectivizing myself, I have since known with my eyes open much wider on all things, that the life we unfurl can also reveal joy. If the art of an artist is the song of his life, serious or sad melody, I had to offer a gay note through color; I will tell about it another time.

If I stopped writing here, I might offer this piece as a kind of introduction to my catalogue. At this moment the publishers Artz and DeBois from the Hague give me profound satisfaction in the publication of my complete graphic work. It is an ensemble of works of varied achievement, where several are seeds, first attempts of which the second sap has flowered in a drawing which is not there—and flowered more happily perhaps: a drawing which by necessity came out of the studio before being transmitted to the stone. There are, therefore, approximately 500 that stray and go through the world according to their destiny. I recommend them to those who love my lithographs. Charcoal, that light material that a breath could take away, allowed me the rapidity of gestation amenable to the docile and easy expression of feeling. I would like it to be understood in leafing through the series: the tenacity that I have used to know what the beautiful granite of Munich could supply and multiply for the utmost brilliance of the print in the expressive mode. There are several proofs whose graphic result will doubtless demonstrate and justify the others, I hope.

One must be modest, therefore, in putting before the eyes of the public the totality of his fruits—always more or less good, according to the years, according to our days.

◆ ◆ ◆

March 15, 1915—*Reply to a pacifist circular from Holland.*

Dear Sir, in response to the request you were good enough to address to me, I will ask you to put yourself in our place through thought.

Please suppose that Holland were invaded and the enemy, after having committed the injustices known to you, is moreover, occupied in destroying, automatically and for no military reasons, some of the most beautiful works of art of your patrimony.

Would you think of expressing wishes for peace? I do not believe it: the hour would seem to you premature.

No: the Germany of today is a dishonored nation without glory, and her dishonor follows the course of progression, the end of which you can guess, will be far from rendering her worthy of the pardon you speak of, or let her enter into the great family of human love and goodness of which we are part, of which you are part and which inspired, Sir, the engaging terms, so noble and lofty, of the confidential circular you communicated to me.

Please understand that I wait to reply to you until that moment when Germany will be punished or defeated, that is to say, when her army will no longer be on the soil of deluded Belgium, deceived but glorious, and when she will no longer be on the soil of France.

For the same reasons, I have not asked those around me, either, to join the initiative you have just taken.

◆ ◆ ◆

One must give to those one admires.

What sweetness, what nobility to do good for the accomplishment of beauty!

It is good that the gift of a work of art leads to the benefit of charity. But (in order not to bring confusion to our feelings) one should not use the idea of brotherhood to urge us to assist artists. Certain words have a kind of creative power that can mislead consciousness if they are poorly understood. When you think this over, you see that the idea of fraternity cannot rise from the artists taken as a community.

There where desire lies, our weakness is exposed. Envy is the needle magnetised toward the strongest. One must then be rich enough to find in the folds of his being the freedom inscribed in this verse and song of the Holy One: "It is better to follow our own law, though imperfect, rather than the law of others, though better."

Politicians of Parliament obey in darkness the directions of their party. War gave them light. Through the threat of their total disappearance, they have suddenly seen the French reality, that is to say, the most general reason for their mandates, whence comes their unexpected union to fashion a law of defence.

How great it would be to see all the laws thus voted unanimously!

Belonging to a party is to get several people together to coerce the liberty of others and coerce oneself.

Belonging to a party is to enter an impasse. No other issue but one's own liberty, mute and enclosed.

Art criticism is not creative. The artist does not retain any benefit from it: he is its source. He is the active generator, who goes, follows his way, evolves according to his secret intuition.

◆ ◆ ◆

Schumann

"Be a noble artist," Schumann said, "and all the rest will be given to you." It is because he was noble himself if one understands by "noble" the absolute unselfishness, generosity, expansion and the vivid exuberance of a full and strong soul. Schumann has *given* his fruit; he has given it, as the apple-tree gives apples, without personal wishes, and without regrets. He has given his heart and his thought, his works, his life in the same way as those who suffer for others, and therein lies the supreme grace, the characteristic sign of profound genius. One cannot say this about everybody; one could not say this about somebody like Berlioz, for example, who could not open his heart except in continuous recriminations. Follow him in his anxious life, in his torment, and you will see that all his unhappiness has its source in this longing for glory which haunted him unceasingly from his earliest beginnings.

He complains, he calls out everywhere for laurels with passion, with the vehemence of bitterness; he is an aristocrat. He will never be truly loved by the people who have a very sure, very fine sense to recognize those who love them. He was seen traveling all over Europe and gathering everywhere enthusiastic approval; he was called upon and praised by princes as far away as St. Petersburg; the successes he obtained never established him outside his country, which he loves, because he is French, essentially French and he constantly comes back with the hope of receiving the homage due him, that he awaits in vain from his country.

One looks nonetheless in vain in his writings for a sign of submission to his destiny. He speaks in one of his letters about a certain "general and particular" vengeance, as if the spontaneous cheering of an assembly of 2000 people was the payment of a debt owed to him. "It is beautiful, it is sublime," he cried out, listening for the first time to his opera *The Trojans* and he burst into tears, but the tears did not appease him at all.

Berlioz was a great artist, but I prefer Schumann, Beethoven, because they are of the common people. Schumann is almost a great man. The democratic nature also has its nobility; one would look in vain for these traits in Berlioz. He is everywhere himself, sarcastic, haughty and egotistical; it is really incomprehensible in the author of the *Requiem*, and of so many works where the tender and passionate feelings of love were so deeply expressed. He suffered, and doubtlessly suffered greatly, and I refuse to give him the mark of love and veneration which one gives so promptly to a great man. He was a martyr, Schumann a poet.

(December, 1915)

◆ ◆ ◆

Berlioz

A work of art blossoms only at its hour. To be understood it has its proper time: this master made his work too early, this other too late; it is rare that a happy glory grows freely for a genius, especially in our time where each artist, each thinker seeks his own way and has no other initiator of his work than himself.

How many thoughts crowd into my mind in support of this affirmation, which comes first and with sadness under my pen; how many painful careers have we not seen in this century,

118

accomplished with pain and good faith through common contempt and indifference; how many strivings and how many tears, what a difficult fight for the truth.

Let us leave the sad vicissitudes and resentments that a careful study of our time will, perhaps, erase; would it be a necessary law, a fatal and superior law, that makes us condemn today what we will adore tomorrow? Must generations succeed each other thus, greedy, superficial and noisy, and the gentle and deep spirits who, by love and honesty scrutinize the heart of things, should they be condemned, whatever they want, whatever they do, to live only with bitterness?

Berlioz was one of them.

His definition: music is the expression of a passionate and miserable soul.

(April 4, 1878)

◆ ◆ ◆

Fromentin

I went to visit Fromentin, who is a worldly man: with all the impassive, formal kindness and politeness. I went to him on a sorrowful day when I sought the heart of an artist, a cordial hand. But I saw nothing but a bizarre being, unsteady, with an untrustworthy heart, difficult to understand: yet, the author of *Dominique*! I had seen him in this novel; I have vaguely yet certainly recognized him. He paid me pretty compliments, holding out his hand to me—still a worldly hand—fine, aristocratic, a hand of good breeding.

When he learned that I also was a painter, he suddenly looked at me straight in the eye saying: "What? We are colleagues!" He repeated these words several times, after which he remained silent and kept his gaze fixed on me, deeply observant and curious, shrewd, horribly embarrassing.

Then he also told me to come back, assuring me that my name would be among the privileged or friends, who enter his home at any hour. But I never returned. I missed there, something I cannot explain. How much I prefer the simple and

119

confident access of the good Chintreuil.

(June, 1868)

◆ ◆ ◆

Millet

Millet's great originality consists of the good fortune he had
to develop two faculties rarely found together in the same man,
and apparently contradictory: he was a painter and a thinker. I
mean specifically a painter in the manner of the Spanish, Dutch,
and some contemporary French artists; those, in a word, who
feel nature directly and render her with full sensitivity to others
through the palette and tonality. This exquisite sensuality is a
rare gift which brings infinite enjoyment to the observer of the
phenomena of the outdoors, but which also has the danger of
carrying him to pure contemplation and of absorbing and
completely erasing the thinking being who might give himself
up to it beyond all measure. The predominance of this faculty
makes a painter. Velasquez, for example, is the highest manifestation of this. It is he who, with extreme skillfullness, I could
even say virtuosity, surrendered himself most completely to the
immediate reproduction of the object; he seems to have made
the artist a passive and irresponsible being who leaves to nature
the concern for speech. It is the same with the Dutch, with
whom the longing for simple reproduction brought forth un-
equalled craftsmen whose works are models of this type. It is
also the same with some contemporary painters who call
themselves, after Courbet, "*intransigents*" or "*impressionists*" and
who, experimenting outdoors in full *daylight*, with the set
purpose of modelling only between extreme values brought
closely together, found in color new and unforeseen delicacies.

But the most beautiful works of these workers will never be
worth in quality the smallest scrawl of Albrecht Dürer, who
bequeathed to us his very thought, the life of his soul, everything
which is not the sensuality of which I spoke before, but which
is still very human, very vivid.

Michelangelo also is not a painter in the sense we indicate

here; neither is Da Vinci. These names, are they not among the very first in art! Rembrandt was also wonderfully gifted in giving life to his dream through chiaroscuro. And Millet takes after this master.

As in him, the poet was never absorbed by the painter, he had his vision. He looked for and found in the "*plein-air*" an absolutely new world. He gave moral life to clouds. Trees and all the inanimate nature of the countryside live in the life of man. There is a beautiful drawing by him which fully gives the idea of his ideal; it is of two children near a hillock, one is knitting, the other is looking very high in the bright sky toward I don't know what phenomenon, perhaps to the flight of some bird. There is on this page a poetry truly new.

If one notices now that throughout his whole life this master represented the French peasant, that is to say, the Frenchman in the passive work of agriculture, one could not consider him a very self-conscious thinker, who passed judgment on his entire life. There are good grounds for reflection in the study of his work.

(April 23, 1878)

◆ ◆ ◆

Ingres

Ingres was not of his time; his spirit is sterile. The sight of his works, far from amplifying our moral strength, lets us placidly get back to the stream of our bourgeois life, without being in the slightest way touched or modified by it. They are not true works of art, whose virtue is to increase our moral strength or their superior influence.

Such is modern work: the smallest scrawl by Delacroix, by Rembrandt, by Albrecht Dürer makes us creative, makes us get back to work all the same: one could say it is life itself that they communicate, that they transmit to us; and therein is the decisive result, the *supreme range*. Whoever acts in this way upon others has genius, whatever may be the nature of actions exercised by him, by word, by writing, even by his presence.

Ingres is an honest disciple serving masters of another age. As

121

he is lacking in reality and in vital warmth (properly so called), he has the chance of enduring only in the tempered spheres of that banal and bored world which admires traditional beauty on the faith of others, and by the spirit of conservatism as well. In France, he will always represent, like Poussin, like David and others of this nature, the haughty and paternal incarnation of official art. He will remain in the schools: every time the rhetoricians speak from the height of their professorial chair about the origins and traditions of pagan art, his name will be pronounced.

They say he is one of those who live, but this is debatable; if he is one of those who do not animate others, he therefore does not live: it is death itself.

Moreover, what then, is this life of works about which they speak in certain places with a dogmatic tone? What is immortality?

Immortality is nothing but the bloom of the rare flower whose seed is at the heart of all beauty; it is praise, admiration, the springing up of the divine seeds contained in a little bit of matter. People, through the flow of time, make the flowering more or less beautiful. The issue is only to leave to them works which they see, which they love, consult, scrutinize with anxiety at the hours of love and research. Supreme strength which attracts and uplifts them and which they develop afterwards, drawing out of it a new life, which they will put into new works.

Just next door, at this time, is a school, envious keeper of the principles of judgment; what do I say? dark, mournful headquarters, where they eradicate those precious seeds. It has formulas for death which it conserves and transfers unceasingly to the students it educates and maintains for its own purpose. In these false temples, great false gods are praised to the skies, Ingres always, the disciple who follows behind. Sentences are engraved in golden letters on marble, obstinately hollow and as empty as this one: *drawing* is the *honesty of art*, words full of pomposity pronounced by those hackneyed persons who come with their stiff airs into these pious dens. What does honesty have to do with it?

Perhaps they wanted to speak about the dogma of the so called classical drawing that is taught there. The study of

Michelangelo, of Rembrandt, of Albrecht Dürer is forbidden there. They did not make honest art, it is dishonest to create, to have genius, and furthermore, to be a prophet.

It was said that these schools and the dead fruits they brought forth are useful. One more question: what does usefulness have to do with it? is beauty useful? No. Is usefulness beautiful? No. A shoe is not beautiful, neither is bread.

(April, 1878)

◆ ◆ ◆

Cazin

The painting *Ismail* is now in the Luxembourg. It was at the Salon of 1879 that the name of Cazin was seen for the first time. He signed an allegory of *Art* whose conception was strange and new, and a *Flight into Egypt*, a sort of twilight landscape painted in wax, which was placed high in the room of drawings where the only visitors are indifference or solitude.

The soft mysterious feeling which seemed to be imprinted could make one believe in the presence of a primitive painting lost among ours. It surprised, and without any artifice gave harmoniously the flavor of a distant mentality, like a melody by Berlioz in a concert of military music: the same penetrating fragility, tender spirituality, and the same power of legendary evocation. It was indeed the prelude or rather the promise of other paintings that this new talent would give later, as for since then, relatively serious, more sure works, have come again, all marked by the same moral savor. They now give the assurance of a career that the painter will accomplish for the enjoyment of delicate spirits, who praise it and now expect it.

Those who above all seek the pleasure of the eye will not stop long before those canvases, so tempered, a little prudish . . . where portions of reality of sensuality are measured out, and not in order to cause harm to the light idealism inspired in us. They will go before works of another sort, applauding the results of a naturalism which is useful for art, and is its primary value, but is secondary when taken as an aim and not as a means; two faces of the truth which always will be opposed and complementary: here substances, visible reality, sensitive, concrete, without which all conception remains in a state of abstraction and thus of creative palpitation; there the imagination itself, wide perspectives open to the unforeseen of our dreams, without which the work of art has neither aim nor scope. Cazin doubtless does not ignore this, as he keeps—conscious and prophetic artist that he is—true balance in the center of these two worlds of which he has a clear view, without being absorbed too closely by external nature, without being out of depth either in concepts and inventions, where many lofty spirits were lost.

What should be appreciated in those new works is the extent, the maturity of the fruit in its accomplishment. Recent pastels reveal their author to be a skillful and rare worker. *Night* is the simple representation of a hovel next to a garden under a somber sky where a few pale stars sparkle. A ray of moonlight with its mystery falls on the roof, on the door a human being will knock in the half-light, imperceptible yet present. Nothing is simpler and yet newer, more poetic than his modest little outline which suggests the cradling rhythm of a beautiful verse. The author perhaps has illustrated here a verse of the Song of Solomon: "I was asleep, but my heart was on the watch, here is the voice of my beloved, who knocked saying: 'Open the door to me, my sister, my great friend, my dove, my perfect one, as my head is full of dew and my hair of drops of the night.'" This is a page from the Bible, with its remote poetry, its simple lines, its great forgotten style: it echoes in an art whose secret Cazin sometimes holds.

Here is the opportunity for meditation on works that are nothing but historical landscapes, so truly sincere as to prove supremely that the stylistic landscape is a fashion, a traditional form of our pictorial art, which is legitimate and renewable, when asserted by favorable faculties.

Look also at the *The Road* and let us understand that it is by no means a question of the path in the outskirts bordered by farms, where one goes for a Sunday walk. The path he painted is not *a* path: that is to say, a given fact taken in a general sense. The path climbs to a little hill under an azure sky full of vivid activity and light. A purely literary eye would see in this rising path the symbol and image of life where the organic line will be lost in the evening sky. The painter, who has presented it so well, climbed the happy hill beyond which is the sky of reward; he represented it brilliant and rosy, like an image of his success.

The characteristic trait of his good works and those that I have pointed out is that they are beyond space and time. And yet they are deeply true; their author surely has not seen this path; however, he gave to it a resemblance to those we see everywhere: here is true and lofty art and it is to resolve an unusual problem, which is solved only by highly gifted artists.

Cazin is a painter-poet: he proceeds as much by sensitivity as by reason. The poetry he reveals is so sure, so tender and so propitious in awakening in us distant and mysterious reminiscences that it has the power to make us indifferent from now on to many works called "artistic" and which are indeed skillful, extremely skillful, but do not have the supreme and decisive power of *the scope* of the essential transmission. There will be much to say about the sudden apparition at this hour of naturalism, of this sort of meaning in painting, so particularly spiritualistic, although so modern, which profits so well and with so much discretion and moderation from recent acquisitions in the art of painting: the *open-air*, this new manner of which so much has been said; he feels it, penetrates it, and uses it marvelously; the main law of complementary colors asserted and developed by Delacroix is not unknown to him, for he draws from it delicate and fine effects, happily combined. I do not speak here about the *line*, this abstraction, this invisible stroke, on which all lofty work rests, and for which he has a fine and measured sense.

(1881)

◆　◆　◆

Through a need for classification, one easily allows oneself to designate artists by schools, by opposite groups of colorists or draughtsmen; their works must also be of history, genre scenes, landscape, still life, or whatever, do I know? It would be difficult to place Cazin among one or the other, to establish that he is rather this than that: he is himself, very simply, himself and that is all.

Let us speak no more either of strictness or impressionism; one has even joked sometimes about "luminism," "sensationism." There should be found a definite and lasting term for qualifying the *free* artist who obeys his instinct and his reason only.

Cazin has no apotheosis. This is because his success came too late to him.

I saw one day outdoors, a man whose appearance impressed me; he looked contrained, anxious, hugging the walls. His eye scanned the street's horizon as if he were looking for someone in the distance. This obstinate observation of distant things identified him for me, it was he. High forehead, hard profile, willful mouth, blond hair like in his painting. He is nevertheless powerful; you feel somebody under this shell.

Far from naturalism, Cazin dresses the worker in clothes other than those of today; he dresses him out of place and for all time.

Cazin, Puvis are the only ones who make us forget the street.

It is not because a sect believes that it has discovered painting by looking at trees, peasants, cattle, that it should be forbidden to look at life manifesting itself. Look at Cazin and the tree, the blossom, the ground, the cottage, the path, as well as at the smallest blade of grass that borders it; all reveal the thinking being who crosses it and breathes there. Man is in his landscape, he was living there.

The artist must have a heart that dominates his own heart, aims, his own manner of facing human matters; without the seriousness of life, the work does not have it either.

Here is *Dead Town*, a deserted place where no human being appears. It has rained, streams pour out rushing water in which is reflected a large opening of sky, some pale stars, heavy clouds which will pass; in the calm of the evening and the twilight, fires are lighted here and there behind the window panes of closed and sad houses. One is far away, in lonely country, outside the world where the soul is buried in an extinguished life, a small vehicle at rest testifies that one has moved during the day, traveled, received something from the neighborhood. There is all the silence of a lost country, the poverty of a rural evening, the mournful torpor of the motionless.

This work is a cruel truth; a reproach: the moralist could see there a striking picture of an ankylosed province. It is also a poem because it awakens in us an incalculable world of reveries and reminiscenses, like the feeling of a former time. The opposite of contemporary works, its effect is such that the sensation it produces remains a long time alone in us, mistress and dominant, like the favorite melody one hums when leaving a concert.

(February, 1883)

* * *

Meissonier

The painting of Meissonier is one of the most beautiful of the day. You say that it lacks perspective? that is true, but you will note that primitive painters do not have it either. At the close of an era, we come back to the processes of its beginnings. There is a great power of imitation and representation in this work. If the backgrounds and distances are formed and achieved in the same way as the objects and persons of the foreground, it is because the author has done nothing but obey a law of his nature, which brings him always to see nature in the most minute detail and thus with the faithfulness of photography. He has conceived, sustained, worked on, and finished this painting of Waterloo, for years; I affirm that the author has put in this canvas all the painterly skillfulness of his talent.

(*Conversation with Chenavard*)

* * *

Chintreuil and Prud'hon

How many thoughts awaken in me at the hour when those two masters have their works brought together at the same time and side by side in a serious exhibition. Two rather personal and private collections, joined at the Beaux-Arts thanks to a generous and patriotic friendship, attract, but a little too late, the elite of collectors toward two geniuses united by a common aspect of their destinies. You cannot help but meditate upon the common fate of those two men of genius, almost unrecognized during their lives, appreciated after their death in the first beginnings of their glory. Prud'hon was indeed contested during his life; his spirit so tender and impassioned was eclipsed during the First Empire by the scholastic and pedantic uproar of the school where David excelled with all the brilliance and author-ity of a great celebrity. Who could read as we see it now in those pages so sincerely animated, who could see then the loving and sweet grace contained in those drawings, which appeared so simple, mostly lithographs at a moment when lithography was only in its cradle? Indeed, the official painters of those times would have smiled oddly if somebody came to tell them that a hundred years later their works would be ridiculously old-fashioned, those flat nudes falsely imitating the antique, while the marbles newly discovered, had not yet revealed their prime beauty. They would have smiled, and conscientiously, if the helmets, the tunics, all the antique apparel had been despised, cast off, in favor of the simple expression of a soul sincerely impassioned by love, grace, beauty, as revealed by antiquity young and divine: eternal love.

Indeed, destiny unrolls thus for each thing, with a logic and assurance of which the artist is not always aware; Prud'hon's contemporaries did not see there as clearly as he; he alone, by the docility of his artist's conscience and by the law that soars over all things, probably felt that his art was not on the wrong path.

We think the same of Chintreuil, that severe and pure artist, whose fate united him, for a moment, with the artist we have just spoken about. As for Prud'hon, the hour had not come for this tender and gentle genius who reveals himself simply in a fully reserved form, whose deep and passionate modesty finds an echo only in a few chosen souls.

Chintreuil had actually a retiring and austere life. Success never had for him the great burst which brought forth some talents more externalized and virile for whom the crowd seems not to care. He is sheltered from those violent reactions which, in our day, have placed certain names too low and certain others too high. His fame, like his work, appears slowly, feebly and seems to fear the noise of full daylight. It makes its way thus, without emphasis to assert itself for a longer time, and more strongly. It is thus for all who call him to join them in the austere ways of a strict conscience and its rigid application.

◆   ◆   ◆

Fantin-Latour

Fantin-Latour, more austere, more chaste and also more independent because of the origins of his first studies, is nevertheless the one who provides the closed, worldly people all the necessary talent needed to paint the dress, the hat, the glove, the fan, the carpet or rare flowers. He doubtless leans upon the example of the Dutch masters who also paint the costumes of their contemporaries, forgetting that in the Low Countries of former times, the life, political circumstances, and morals of the people of this republic assured in advance each model who posed, the sincerity and the naturalness of an instinctive look.

The costumes painted by Rembrandt of the rich as well as of the poor were living and expressive covers, not a fold of which hid the essence of the man who wore them; coats, felt hats, necklaces, doublets were always living clothes. Could we say the same about contemporary portraits? No. And yet in those polished fields drawn by Millet, human and grotesque beings raise their picturesque, epic silhouettes, with a strictness of line and plasticity which will never teach us enough. (Their costumes will never be out of fashion.)

Fantin-Latour is not in the least a discerning disciple of Delacroix, when the latter is rational, sensual. His palette, which is the one true palette, is a perfect keyboard that provides all degrees of the colors admirable for painting the freshness of flowers, the brilliance of fabrics; perhaps not very complete when he must be asked for the fundamental *gray* which differentiates the masters, expresses them and is the soul of all color.

Laborious and careful research led this artist to attempt the interpretation of music through painting, forgetting that no color can render the musical world which is uniquely and deeply internal and without any support from real nature. Not having succeeded, he doubtless takes revenge in discharging his sorrows through lithography in pale, soft sketches on the poems of the musician, Wagner. But whether he draws out of the "libretti" of Brahms, Schumann, or Berlioz, it is always the expression of a vague German sentimentality that is not new for us and that needs to be given with less emphasis. One cannot abolish contradictory qualities. This one whose exquisite *Dead Flowers* we have seen does not know how to organize his painting. If you change, in your mind, the placement of a figure, of an object, his painting is no less relatively good. He only organizes colors, pink, blue, green, yellow, etc.

Aerial perspective is not so familiar to him; his domain, his universe remains quartered in a space of three meters, before a wall where stand Mme. X, M. Y, with a hat on the head. Landscape is unknown to him; he fails with a surprising inability when he has to paint a horizon. (It is an oblivion of the essential world, which is no less important among musicians.) It is in vain that the beautiful works of Cazin, which he imitates, haunt him in his dreams: he is searching uselessly for what the other found at birth.

"To make copies is the greatest happiness I know," he said to a person who preferred the study of the antique to painting. He answered that this passion for Greek marble, when it was sincere, only came to the artist later. One could believe that this search for beauty came to haunt this romantic structure. Looking at the last production of this painter, one could see tendencies to simplify that palette originally so luxuriant and exuberant.

Fantin-Latour puts naturalism within the reach of worldly people as did Bastien Lepage. He makes of the country and the peasant a picture quite decent, bourgeois, presentable, where nothing could shock the view of those who do not live there. Whatever he paints, be it a *woodcutter*, a *beggar*, the spectator will be unaware of the sadness of the condition of those beings, which could be a reproach, and will calmly admire those rags, those wrinkles, that very tiredness which are indeed harmless images. The nature in which he places them is cultivated ground, well cut, fertilized, and which recalls rustic walks of days of leisure; in all this nothing shocking; everything necessary to become soon an official image of the handsome contemporary. He is an intransigent, without the naturalness and sincerity of enthusiasm, a liberal who conserves everything necessary to please and succeed.

(November, 1882)

◆ ◆ ◆

Puvis de Chavannes

During the great epochs, painting was in fresco; but at other times what do we do? We can of course cover the walls with important works; we can also do historical painting: very beautiful pages can be tried in the art of decoration; but one will only be able to succeed in those lofty genres only if he treats his subject with strict modesty, with the sense of sacrifice which imposes on the hand a simplified and concise work. This is what Puvis de Chavannes knows and it is for this reason that he could, without ever having deviated from his choice, succeed so well in painting on stone; a daring and bold task toward which the critic was too harsh.

One will not fully understand the work of this master without adopting his own point of view, which is unquestionably the following: modeling the human figure and the trees and all things as if they were in the tenth, the twentieth plane; therein lies the key to his work.

Look at an object which is far away and see how the lines become simplified, how the planes diminish, how the difference between values is hardly perceptible. Figures there have a shadow, a light, and the shadow projected by the bodies is not visible. At the horizon the mountains will be nothing more than an edge, which will stand out sharply against the sky line like a stage set.

Puvis de Chavannes is farsighted in his abstractions: he must have reflected for a long time before starting to paint and to find his way, a way debated about as are all those which disclose a personal intelligence. He has done well to find it, nevertheless, and to follow it since he could entrust his spirit to us without any coyness, paint his dream and make, in a word, a work which others imitate and which will remain: he has found his style.

◆　◆　◆

Courbet

A painter who was famous and who for a long time was president of official juries just made a full apology in front of Courbet's paintings exhibited at the Beaux-Arts, quite varied paintings from different periods, which can give a definitive and complete idea of the master. Of course, it will not be that reversal expressed by a person of late talent, which will weigh heavily on the minds of those who judge, nor can it noticeably hasten the hour of justice; because justice, like fame, comes at her hour. Great works transcend time, radiant and peaceful; around them the truth works out slowly through obstacles placed by the events of the moment around their strength, and in spite of meager speeches about error and silliness, they remain, they stay alive, they triumph and assert themselves.

The honest confession of the academician, while making us smile, also arouses sadness: all who suffer, who think, who look to true art as it appears outside of the rules of a school, will regret such reserve expressed about judgements of the past, will stay powerless to prevent errors of the future; it is thus. It is difficult to judge one's contemporaries; perhaps it is impossible to understand them. After all, we live in an artistic atmosphere, through which it is difficult to see clearly what occurs in other areas; posterity, finally, is nothing but the sum of opinions formulated during the continuance of time by isolated and disinterested men, who compare and announce the truth to others, without any envy, without passion, and in defiance of the present.

It is thus that today we can look without too many errors at the work of the great realist who was simply a great painter. Every man who has eyes open on life and sees it palpitating under the skin of things, every man who sees substances and loves them has in the depth of his being a sleeping painter. The will could develop inconsistent faculties in him; circumstances could lead them to atrophy; but the germs will always be alive in him. Courbet evolved powerfully in a unique type of activity. He was sensitive, a delicate viewer of things, joyously amused by magic changes of exterior light. For him, no doubt, the art of painting was a delectation; and as he never painted except out of love and voluptuousness, he was impeccable. Not a square inch of canvas, not an accentuation which could be anything but the exuberant love of color itself, that is, the eternal play of daylight on the day itself, with an exact feeling in every respect.

One would like to see *The Stonebreakers* next to a Titian, which it recalls. Same fullness, same force, no nobility, it is true, but what an ardor in this nature, colored to its zenith and congested, so to speak. The sun falls straight and directly on this joyless road where the work is dreary, almost hopeless. Those two formless things, (two peasants, as La Bruyère would see them) move passively like wooden mechanisms. Not a human face, gazes are hidden: here is the unconscious and automatic torpor of life, the paralysis, the deep and fatal humiliation of the enchained beast. As in Rembrandt, there are deep and humanitarian implications, a supreme mockery arises here, in the form of a lesson. Only a human reality, even a fortuitous one, can contain a reproach beyond time and can participate by enduring in the infinite march toward the better. The question is that it was caught in the act by some incorrigible child, like humanity, tired of her pose, sometimes knowingly lets him pass through the sieve of the Rule. The divine babies who do not have the middle years to grow up, become men and even great men, while the others move toward the grave, impotent, conquered, disarmed, debased; this is justice. M. Robert Fleury is dying and ends honestly; he said of the master whom he had formerly denied and contested, "He is a great painter." This is the opinion of those who will rise in the near future to exalt and elevate the name of Courbet through the difficult life that the work of art encounters in posterity.

Courbet was tall, powerful. Large and friendly eyes lit up his good-natured face where pride, in flashes, evoked vivacity. "I will take up a gun in spite of my genius," he said, at the time of war, at the very hour the enemy invaded. Compliments transformed him, dominated him; prizes made him like a child being led by the hand.

(May, 1882)

◆ ◆ ◆

Reflections on an Exhibition of the Impressionists

It is to be feared that Berthe Morisot has already given the full extent of her talent; she is like a flower which has given its perfume and which fades, alas, like all exquisite and short-lived blossoms. The only woman, perhaps, who has the gifts of a painter. She has provided several charming and supremely distinguished notes in this concert of diehards who now group solely under the banner of independent artists. There remains, however, in Mme. Berthe Morisot the marks of an early artistic education, which clearly separates her from M. Degas, from this coterie of artists whose formulas and precepts were never plainly stated. Look at those watercolors, so vividly produced, those extremely subtle and feminine strokes; they are sustained by indications, by linear intentions, which give a finer, more delicately formed accent to those charming works than to those by others.

This is not to deny all the legitimacy of those workers who never forget to place on the pediment of their temple (if there is a temple): *exhibition of painting*. This emphasis, a little pretentiously parvenu, is permitted to them, if one compares it to so many others who are almost nothing and who fill the official galleries with their sad and distressing productions. What is their goal, their aim?

They only seek to disengage color or light from the last bonds of classical painting. Classical themselves, since, as they give in to this external ideal of concrete painting, they hope to be able to place the essence of painting on the true field of *tone* taken for its own sake. The germs of this manner of understanding the beautiful art of painting are in the latest works of Corot, of Millet. They attain, without opposing surfaces, without organizing planes, a vibration of tone seen by the juxtaposition of a gray which vanishes at a distance and which produces a result only a few steps away from the frame. A method of painting quite justified in so far as it concerns above all the representation of external things under the open sky. I do not believe that all that palpitates behind the brow of a man who listens to himself, communes with himself, I do not believe that *thought* considered in its specificity, has much to gain of set purpose in watching only what happens outside our dwellings. The expression of life can appear differently only in light and shade. Thinkers love shade, they walk in it, they delight in it as if their brains had found their *element* there. Everything considered, those estimable painters will not sow fruitful fields in the rich domain of art. "Man is a thinking being." Man will always be there in time, in eternity, and all that belongs to light will not be able to avert him. The future, on the contrary, belongs to the subjective world.

M. Degas, surely the greatest artist of this group, is a Daumier holding his palette. It is the same deep and true study of Parisian life.

(April 10, 1880)

◆　◆　◆

Rodolphe Bresdin

We are sometimes too forgetful of men of value whom we have the good fortune to meet: true talent is not always surrounded by the consideration it deserves. Wherever thought asserts itself, without the support of a militant fight, wihout the strong contradictions of the animated consent of enthusiasm, one could say that the man of value receives in small measure the reward for his generous endeavors. That is why in his own country, the genius often succumbs for want of opponents, to fight him, or friends to exalt him. The talent which comes from far, already crowned by prestige and established reputation, probably attains renown more easily; but what obstacles, what difficulties he meets in our improvidence, in the inexperience of some judges too eager to explain him prior to having understood him!

If knowledge sometimes betrays us, if the most beautiful side of talent is overlooked by us, often for what it has that is the most precious and powerful, it is above all when it appears in a rather free and new way. M. Bresdin, though highly appreciated by a small circle of amateurs whose admiration has the best motives, did not obtain in Bordeaux the place and fame he deserves. This name, though preceded by a justly acquired reputation and already pointed out by some authorized pens, did not evoke the surprise that should happen for a talent so singular and so new. Yet, let us say sincerely, this is an artist of fine and good breeding: in his strong individuality, in his work, so varied and at the same time so rich, fertile and deep-rooted, one recognizes the true mark of the artist of high rank and of the best family; it is on those grounds particularly that he appeals to the attention of art lovers smitten with new beauties, rare perfumes, to all those, finally, who, tired by insipid imitations, seek art in its unknown and unexplored paths.

Three methods serve alternatively the singular manifestation: the pen-drawing on stone, the etching and the pen-drawing, a quite new genre which he alone practices and of which he is, we can say, the creator. His most famous work is a large drawing on stone known as *The Good Samaritan*. Strange creation. It is useful to note here that it was not the artist's goal to represent a landscape that we see everyday from our window; from that point of view this work could certainly be considered imperfect because none of our contemporaries could have been inspired more outside of the manner of imitation. What he wanted, what he sought was only to initiate us into the impressions of his own dream. Mystic dream and deeply strange, it is true, anxious and vague reverie, but what does it matter? Is the ideal precise? Does not art, on the contrary, draw all the forces of its eloquence, its brilliance, its mightiness in matters which leave to the imagination the trouble of defining them?

The conception and research of the elements able to formulate it, to strike, to seize our disconcerted imagination, is the only theory which presided over this work if, at least, the liberty of fantasy obeys any law. Considered thus, this work has really reached its goal, because no one leaves in our spirit a mark as strong as this one, a stamp as vivid, of such a great originality.

You can add to this work *The Good Samaritan, The Holy Family*, done in the same method, but of smaller dimensions, which better suit this genre of drawings, where detail is so minutely observed. This work is more complete, richer, more sincere in its expression. Nothing could be more naive, more touching than this little page, certainly created in a moment of particularly happy excitement, of abandon to the ideal. Delicate and fine exploration of detail, richness of arrangement and yet sober, simple in effect.

Such is the high aesthetic quality of this work, little known, for it became rare, but which will remain, certainly, as the most complete expression of the research of its author. We can also, add the *Comedy of Death*, work of a different scope, less sculptural perhaps, but no less interesting. And finally, proofs for a rather important illustration, which the artist could not finish. In the first plates of this special collection, so beyond everything done today, one can draw freely from a real treasure of capricious fantasy.

The etcher is less known. However, it is certainly in this supple and rapid process that the artist found his true element. He knows about all of the resources and all of the tricks. Led by his own temperament and by a rigorous integrity to the most subtle and refined research, one can say that his etchings are nothing but a long succession of attempts made out of the incessant desire to approach perfection. Thus, what diversity, what suppleness of means! He attacks the copper with the confidence of an artist for whom the process has ceased to be rebellious. Because without insisting on this technical skill, which would make him only an artist of second rank, he appeals to a much more important capacity that gives him a unique place among contemporary etchers: he is a creator.

To all of the resources of the subtle and clever practitioner, he joins, moreover, the most lofty qualities of the thinker and the charm of imagination. And, indeed, is there anyone whose fantasies are more unexpected and more varied? Landscapes, seascapes, battles, interiors, the most diversified genre subjects, serve in turn as a pretext for his vagrant imagination to manifest here and there her richest caprices and embellish all objects she meets on the free field she crosses.

It is among the pen-drawings that *The Tartar Family on a Journey*, *The Old Houses*, etc. should be placed. Here the author is the most true. This technique, which allows corrections, permits him also to come closer to nature, for which he always had a humble veneration. It is necessary to note here the error spread by some critics who often said that M. Bresdin was descended too directly from the mystic masters of Germany. Certainly one recognizes in him a fervent communion with Rembrandt and, above all, with Albrecht Dürer.

The love of masters is not a very great fault, and let us not blame archaism too much. When well understood, "archaism" is a sanction. One work of art comes directly from another work of art; if the study of nature gives us the necessary means to express our individuality, if the observance and the patient analysis of reality are the very first elements of our language, it is also true that the love of beauty and the search for beautiful patterns must always maintain our faith. Then, it is not surprising if the fervent disciple sometimes shows a weak image of a god he is trying to meet, whom he worships.

Happy are those who feel worthy enough, strong enough to go without dizziness under the rays of those highly glorious beings surrounded by their devotees and to whom posterity still pays immortal homage, the gift of its most prestigious laurels! Welcome to their fellow! If M. Bresdin has some relationship with those masters, it is remarkable that it is much more through means than through thought; because his personality becomes victorious and alive from a contact that would have crushed a disciple less gifted than he. He has indeed a manner of seeing that no master has taught him.

What actually characterizes him is that which nobody, from

the ancients to the moderns, could have given him; it is this unalterable individuality, it is this singular color which spreads over all his work those strange, mysterious, legendary impressions; it is this free way with nature and which, in the slightest attempts from his hands, reflects an inexpressible sadness. Because, if the artist is unable to reproduce nature directly, if the last student of an academic school would be more fit to minutely represent the objects before his eyes, those objects will still occasionally strike him by their most expressive and lively aspect.

We have certainly seen those strange clouds, those misted skies, so deep, so sorrowful. We know how he turned to his advantage those medleys full of strange things, where the eyes love to hunt thousands of apparitions. Water is for him not the least matter for admiration; it has so much tenderness and mystery. We see that he is a landscape painter; he is therefore modern. It is always under the sky that he places his favorite scenes; witness *The Tartar Family on a Journey*, this page so strongly imbued with sentiment and impressions.

It is also because of a peculiar aspect of the French school that the artist relies upon the thinker. This imagination, still so vehement and so young, seems kept in control and dominated by a constant desire wherein, without his applying reason to it, is revealed the exclusive and imperious character of his inner being. What you find everywhere, almost from the beginning to the end of his oeuvre, is a man in love with solitude, fleeing the world, fleeing distractedly under a countryless sky, in the distress of a hopeless and endless banishment. This dream, this constant anxiety takes the most diversified aspects. Sometimes in the image of the divine child, in the *Flight Into Egypt* he represented so often. Another time, it is an entire family, a legion, an army, an entire tribe fleeing, always fleeing civilized humanity.

This is what characterizes M. Bresdin above all. This is what the masters of the Netherlands or of Germany could not have given to him, because this side of human and philosophical art is a quality which is the pride of the French school.

That is why it is among etchings and original drawings that one should search for the true meaning of this individuality. It is through those three methods that we must study him to be

139

able to understand him well. Thus, if the city is quite willing to keep the memory of this artist, she must choose from among that which gives him the most complete expression and she should, above all, put in this choice all the discernment that such a serious matter, so dear to the true lovers of art, requires.

We often believe that beings who devote themselves to art follow only a frivolous preference or penchant but, if we look more carefully, if our attention becomes more enlightened, we shall then see that it is sometimes the most pure and the most severe share of consciousness.

Therefore, if we really wish to adorn our public collections with works of art worthy of being followed, if we look for these works among the artists of merit who bring new influences to art, we will always find them among those who add to the beauty of talent this laudable disinterestedness that is always accompanied by sincerity.

Those rare natures ask that little should be spoken about them; their only misfortune will be to stay a little too long in the meditation of a silent discretion. Let us go to them; let us try to better understand them through a deeper analysis of their work. But if there is doubt, if there is still hesitation about the exact evaluation of this artist whose works Bordeaux has already possessed for several years, there are, however, some true lovers of art who have not hesitated for a long time in recognizing the considerable importance of this extraordinary personality; we strongly believe that their esteem prepares for him in the future the true approval due him.

◆　◆　◆

Delacroix

1878—Gradually, as he proceeds toward the fulfillment of his work, in the stream of his tumultuous career, he strains more and more to realize his drawing by a more rapid and active representation of the human body. At the beginning, he makes an attentive, necessary, study of the model: the vigorous and powerful relief he obtains shows evidence of it (particularly in

The Boat of Dante), but it is only afterwards that he starts to be concerned about the framework, the so-called structure, and that he looks at man, at what is permanent and essential about him. It seems that it was only at the age of sixty that he possessed a skeleton. He confesses then that if it were possible to begin again the study of painting, he would start with precisely this study. The beautiful pencil drawing he did for the decoration of the Chambre des Députés, the drawing for *The Education of Achilles* proves that he had already a sense of representation of the human body quite different from the one he had in his youth; the movement of life is present, as if it fluttered under a skin of crystal. This is typical of him: as far as he analyzes nature, scrutinizes it, decomposes it, he never for a single moment loses the intense, vibrant feeling he has of life, of passion; he always created; there is his greatness. The vital gift is in him, the continuous motor that leads him from one work to the other, by degrees, until the end.

Is it not the imprint of genius to appear thus among us, all alone, complete, unique, little prince or great king of the kingdom?

An art of this character is rare: when it blooms it cannot appear to us entirely like that. When Delacroix began, *with* power and *in* power, he was far from having found his language, his technique. Everything about him was a surprise: audacity, ardor, orginality, temperament, but nothing yet of what he had to acquire slowly, to give fully his lyric flame. Until the age of thirty he revealed only his struggles and his first extravagances of genius, which surprise, seize, and charm the eye. Of course, we know what an uproar he caused. It is after having seen Morocco that he found himself. There he made exact notes, from nature and, in the multiple and variable impressions of the landscape, documents which he used constantly since. This genius so fiery, so vehement, burning with passion throughout his work, this painter, who set out with a painting of damnation, of plague and revolutionary shocks, is now bound to become calmer for a moment, by treating quieter subjects. His *Jewish Wedding* is a first attempt. It is the first page where this anxious imagination at last takes a rest, finds quiet for itself and meditates upon the powers of the palette and the registration of tones. He will be in full possession of it later in his *Algerian Women in their Quarters*, which can be considered as his masterpiece with regard to the ability to handle prismatic effects by a new art of juxtaposition. This was the concern of the colorist, it was the concern of the *pure* painter who enlarged upon and augmented for posterity the very notion of painting. But there was in him the dramatist as well. He needed, however, to satisfy the effervescence of his imagination and what the reading of the beloved authors of his time suggested to him. It is with them and for them that he created *a means*. He compounds it for the good of his heart and his sensitivity, which palpitates and leaps by reading Shakespeare, Byron. One can see in his *Journal* all the activity of his inventive imagination in a notation of projects he intends to realize.

Everyone knows within the oeuvre of the master the strong and vigorous creation of *Medea*. Lithography almost made her popular. It gives a rather true idea of her; it has her color and her finesse; it conveys with an extreme gentleness this bright and fragrant coloring that time erases so quickly and those who have it can consider it a precious reproduction.

But among the works of this master, which are so strangely and diversely controversial, this is surely one of the most popular. It received, at the very moment when Delacroix was the most contested, the approval of the crowd and of almost all "judges" who were opposed to this new manner of understanding art.

Those who know his work see that he operates always in two different ways, and in some sense in two different states of spirit which apparently are contradictory and seem to void each other. Indeed, he sometimes succumbs to the pleasure of painting, he charms the eye, he represents the luminous life, the brilliance of fabrics and, like Veronese, he makes a page of painting, pure painting, where the only passion which enlivens him is the one he has for his palette.

On the other hand, he creates under power of a most intense feeling after silent readings, that fill his soul with fire. That muse is the one to which he is listening above all in his quiet hours;

she is always present, his work testifies to it, and it is this one which, in our way of seeing, will occupy us unceasingly.

We have said that he seriously read contemporary German and English masters. Some minds, perhaps too subtle, have seen in this disposition or set purpose a sign of proceeding from the literary idea or at least from the poetry, already expressed in the letters the outward and main sign of inferiority! Not at all. Delacroix was of his time, that is all. He also knew well that it was necessary above all to captivate the people, this public who is so easily hostile; he sought all his life the language of his moment.

At that hour the Saxon or German influence was excessive. Goethe, Schiller, Heine were read; there was a passion for Byron or Shakespeare. Delacroix was concerned about, and set aside the incomparable critic who doubted and watched so well over this artist; was there not also in him the man who breathed the air of his time? He knew that; he gave up knowingly, he surrendered consciously and willingly to the author of each idea, to the dominant breath of this century, of which he was and of which he wanted to be.

From the beginning, from the moment he painted *The Boat* and *The Damned*, one could expect a different destiny. This page full of the fire of inspiration revealed only the essence of this spirit; the form made it possible to believe in a different future.

Surely this page is modern, because the subject outweighs every other, because the fierce and romantic poetry of hell is entirely here; it is modern because it takes after Dante himself, and his great spirit, the most astonishing perhaps—as the supremacy of Shakespeare is not yet obvious to me—this great Tuscan genius, I say, was mighty enough to be present among us even today. But a scarcely perceptible fact, which no one has seen, should be noted; it is Delacroix's inability to illustrate Dante a second time. Surely, the painters who sent the artist back to his beginnings, telling him that he produced nothing but this page, were not totally and absolutely wrong. Let us put ourselves in their place and we will understand them.

The master is still bound to the past by classical ties. The mode of representation is essentially, formally plastic; he proceeds with flat surfaces; he models, he explores the three-dimensionality of things. The line is sustained; the arrangement is almost sober. What is called *The Piece* is painted for the piece itself; in a word, at the risk of being taken here for an irreverent critic, this work is one that does not reveal anything new, nothing of original invention, except, as we mentioned before, the fierce poetry of Dante, which we can amply rediscover every day at the very source in the old verses of the great poet. Was all this not done to seduce the official painters of his time? And, oh my God, aside from the marvelous and powerful understanding of color and strength of temperament which explodes in it, they could have conceived it themselves.

No, this page is not the most beautiful of the master. It is, at most, the first invention of a genius who is searching for himself and who, upon leaving school, attempts a first affair with the ideal, only to find there the idea of a talented schoolboy, that is all.

A few years more and he will understand that Dante and the Latin world are not his way: he returns to it no more, he secretly has the consciousness that his muscles will no longer carry him on that path, that he will not be strong enough for it, and very soon he will give himself up to his essentially anxious nature, to pure expression, to the representation of the inner life only, and will no longer attempt to struggle in highly modelled form with the ancient masters who surpass him, and he understands finally that his time is the time of pure expression, that Romanticism is only the triumph of feeling over form, and without returns or regrets, he finds his true way, which is expressive color, a color one could call moral color.

He is its creator, and now we are on the ground that we like to give him. He creates expression through color. He makes the palette express what it has not yet said; every object, every stroke made by this rare brush will take on the significance necessary for the whole, and will always represent victoriously the soul of the person on the canvas. Now, as we are in the XIXth century, he takes from the poets of our time the main situations of his canvasses and we will see him express his genial spirit and ardor principally in illustrating them. That is the story of his first conversion.

Color, until now expressing passion and the inner life, strained for balance in its final perfection: the harmony, the necessary juxtaposition, and this supreme harmony is nothing but the unity of color applied to history, to human subjects. In the annals of art it was a discovery of greatest importance but until now only in the domain of landscape. Delacroix has imperiously subordinated it to history; he has made of it a means of the most subtle and the most eloquent expression. This new period, so important for the artist, is what will bring him in the future the awards and approval due him, that glorious and special situation in which are to be found all those who enhance the field of art and who dismiss, only by the power of their genius, the dark cloud which still veiled a part of life for us.

The Chariot of Apollo

This is the work he made in the fullness of his talent and power.

What is its great expression, the most important characteristic? It is the triumph of light over darkness. It is the joy of full daylight opposed to the sadness of night and shadows, like the happiness of feeling better after great distress. He paints every detail in his unique interpretation: Venus is surrounded by tender blue; in a gray cloud, exquisitely tender, cupids fly, unfolding oriental wings. Ceres has all the poetry of our most beautiful landscapes; she is bathed in sunshine. Mercury in his red coat expresses all the pomp of padded well-being and commerce. Mars is of a terrifying violet; his helmet is a bitter red, symbol of war. The painter expresses everything through accessories. Mercury is dark, and all of the suffocating part is even less clearly rendered in the foaming monster, in the superb body of the reclining nymph; one of the most beautiful pieces from his hand in his late style, in its indefinable scale, in those sickly tones which carry the idea of death.

This work is so powerful, so strong because it is new, a whole poem, a symphony. The attribute which defines each god becomes useless, so much does the color undertake to say all and to say it properly; the rest of tradition that he still maintains for clarification is useless.

It is in this way that he still proceeds when working on the

145

small cupola of the Senate and on most of his easel paintings.

Let us compare now, in our minds, a painting of the old school, *The Wedding at Cana* for example, with this essentially new page. Can we find there a space similarly important, given to the idea? No. Venice, Parma, Verona have seen color only from the material side. Delacroix touches at moral color, human color; this is his oeuvre and his claim to posterity.

We cannot guess if this great poet attained perfection; let us say that the daring artist who enhanced and led the ideal in painting was not able from the very first to reach the utmost perfect expression; he obeyed thus the law that directs all innovators. Artists who approach perfection do not have many ideas. There are no examples to be given in the history of art. Delacroix thinks the Ninth Symphony is not perfect; there is no link between the introduction of the voices and the feeling which penetrates it; if it reaches perfection, let us then say that music, that art protected by a sovereign and superior muse, does not have to combine new forms in the more difficult and more rigorous media of the visual arts.

Let us say, without in any way diminishing the idea we have about his high mission, Delacroix should not reach perfection. But this does not prevent us from blaming, without regret, the past of the so-called colorists; the young artists who are affected and enthusiastic in the presence of the master, who should go to the Louvre, only there until now to seek the force of art that is merely representational and that reached with Leonardo, it is true, the summit of beauty in its most essential expression. But our muscles now are not strong enough to recapture this Italian art and express it in the way it was done by these passionate, and highly active people. We shall feel anxious: everything takes us there; music which is now popular will soon commit a supreme blow to the visual arts. No salvation outside of the way followed by the great master about whom we are talking here.

If we have to take advantage of the transformations by the naturalistic school—a school which in my opinion does nothing but continue the classical school—let us at least seek to give to the color which is *seen*, the supreme and pure beauty of the color which is *sensed*: all of modern art is there; nothing great,

146

beautiful, deep can be transmitted in another manner .... I do not believe a return to the past is possible, except after an invasion of a barbarian race, the Russians for example, and fortunately, we will not see this.

Mutual Exaltation of Colors or the Simultaneous Contrast

If complementaries are taken at equal value, the human eye will not be able to endure the sight. The mixture of blue and orange in equal quantities: colorless gray.

But if two complementaries are mixed together in unequal proportion they will be destroyed only partially, and this will give a fractional tone that will be a variety of gray. Thus, new contrasts could be born from the juxtaposition of two complementaries where one is pure and the other fractional. If this struggle is not balanced, one of those two colors will win out and the intensity of the dominant will not prevent the chord of the two. Now, if similar colors are in a pure state but of varying degrees of energy—for example dark blue and light blue—we will get another result that will contain a contrast of the difference of intensity and harmony through the similarity of the colors.

Finally, if two similar colors are placed side by side, one in a pure state, the other fractional—for example pure blue and blue-gray—the result will be another kind of contrast that will be analagously moderate. We can see, then, that means, different but equally unfailing, might exist to fortify, sustain, mitigate and neutralize the impression of a color by operating with what is next to it and what is not it.

One of the utmost precious resources is the insertion of black and white. Black and white are, so to say, non-colors that help, by distinguishing the others, to be restful to the eye, to refresh it, just when it could be tired by extreme variety as well as by extreme magnificence. According to the proportions given to them, according to the places they are used, white and black attenuate or heighten the adjacent tones; sometimes the character of white in a sinister painting is similar to that of a drum struck in a full orchestra. At another time, white can be used to correct what could be brutal in the contiguity of two bold colors such as red and blue.

Modulation of colors—The main colors come to us from the Orient. The shudder of the colored surface by tone over tone is *the resonant tone.*

Optical mixture—Two colors put side by side or superimposed in certain proportions (that is, according to the limit of each) will bring up a third color which our eyes will perceive at a distance, without the weaver or painter prescribing it. This third color is the result that the artist has foreseen, and which is born from the optical mixture (or the mutual reactions of one tone on the other). For example: *The Cupola* at the Luxembourg: a semi-nude woman seated in the shade; *Algerian Women*: a shirt strewn with little flowers. The walls are covered by a blue and yellow mosaic with small drawings that compose the great tonality of a green, soft, fresh, indefinable, opening on a bright red. Paving with small flagstones in violet and green that form a mosaic. To magnify and harmonize those colors, he uses all together the contrast of the complementary and the accord of the analogous (in other words, the repetition of a bright tone by the same tone in fractioned state). He uses the action of the whites, the blacks, which function by turn as a foil, a sharpness and a rest; he also uses the modulation of colors and what is called the optical mixture.

For example, the orange bodice of the reclining woman on the divan allows the edge of its lining of blue satin to be seen; the skirt of violet silk, dark and striped with gold. The Negro woman wears a light blue bolero and an orange colored madras, three tones that sustain and emphasize each other to a degree such that the last becomes even more sparkling because the bronzed skin of the woman had to be cut by the colors of the background in order not to be detached from them too jarringly. Those contrasts, one sees, are juxtapositions of complementary and analogous colors.

One must moderate the contrast without destroying it; one

must pacify the tones in putting them together. The woman seated next to the Negress, who has a rose in her hair, wears short-pants of green with a yellow pattern, whereas her silk shirt is of a tone altered through an imperceptible sowing of small green flowers. But it is not only once, but in series that he inserts and interlaces tones, makes them penetrate each other, respond to, mitigate, sustain each other.

Jewish Wedding in Morocco

The warm tone in the shadow and the cold tone in the light produce a particular sensation, that of freshness under the African sky.

◆　◆　◆

When I saw Delacroix in 1859 he was magnificent as a tiger; same pride, same finesse, same power.

It was at an offical ball at the Préfecture where I was told he would attend. My brother Ernest came with me and he didn't know him any more than I did. But by instinct he pointed out to me a person, small in stature, aristocratic, who stood alone before a group of ladies seated in the dancing salon. Long, black hair, sloping shoulders, bent posture. Discretely, we came next to him, and the master, it was he indeed, cast on us this blinking, unique glance that darted more sharply than the light of the chandelier. He was very distinguished. He had the grand'croix (great cross) on his high stand-up collar and from time to time he looked down at it. He was accosted by Auber who introduced to him a very young Princess Bonaparte, "anxious," Auber said "to see a great artist." He shivered, leaned over smiling, and said: "You see he is not very big."

He was of medium height, thin and nervous. We watched him all that evening in the midst of the crowd, and even left at the same time as he, in his steps. We followed him. He crossed nocturnal Paris, alone, his head bent, walking like a cat on the most narrow sidewalks. A poster, which read "tableaux" ("paintings"), attracted his eye; he approached, read, and went away with his dream—I would say, with his obsession. He crossed the city up to the door of an apartment at the rue La Rochefoucauld where he no longer lived. Was it enough diversion from habit! He calmly returned with his thoughts to the small rue Furstemberg, silent street where he lived henceforth.

I passed more than one time, since then, before the modest door where he disappeared that evening and once I even yielded to my pious curiosity about visiting his apartment.

It was a place built like those built in former times; high ceilings, immense, spacious. He built, himself, a studio overlooking the garden, with southern light from above. I looked with veneration at those memorable places where the master spent the end of his life. Full light tempered by a shade entered abundantly into the spacious room, where I would have wished to see ardent works come to life again like those born from his impassioned hand. It seemed to me that the master's thought was still present and that it accompanied me everywhere.

The small adjoining garden that one reaches after descending from the studio, probably served as a place for him to rest. "Rest often," he used to advise. Everything leads one to believe that he went there to recover strength and ardor in the open air, next to the flowers, under the shadow of the cool bushes still growing and blooming in this enclosure. No outside noises penetrate it. You would think you were far from Paris. Letters from this recluse to a friend far away say that he greatly enjoyed the silence of those quiet places where his last works were conceived and realized.

It is here that death stopped his generous hand. It struck quickly. The short illness which took him away took him in the full maturity of his thought, at the moment he was himself aware of the ardor of his strength and the vigor of his spirit. He was hit by exhaustion as was Raphael, when the last sketches left on his easel overflowed with the passion of his soul which for forty years poured out without failure, without pause.

Romanticism is to be taken and kept as it is. With Delacroix, it is the triumph of movement and passion over form. Where did I read that Victor Hugo, while visiting him one day when the sketch for the *Massacre of the Bishop of Liege* was on the easel, and the poet, not seeing the murderer's weapon very well, asked the painter what he had wanted to do. Delacroix answered, "I wanted to paint the flash of a sword." These remarks on the lips of those two beings is quite evocative....

It seems to me that this master, free, passionate, artist above all and to whom I am indebted for my first awakening and the duration of my own flame, has not yet attained the true place that time owes him. For having made the colors of the prism speak passionately, for having been the first to touch them with genius which gave them the power to express the inner life, he underwent in the time that followed I will not say an eclipse, but an interruption, a delay imposed on his dominance. Naturalism cluttered his path with brushwood. The good or appreciable painters who followed him, who are designated, no one knows why, by the name Impressionists, have given fruits that are much less rare, let us admit it: one must gather them close to the ground, a little low. Those of Eugène Delacroix which grew higher, in the fertile regions of imagination and lyricism, are also the product of human passion. In all he painted, one feels the presence of man. This is not to be neglected. And humanity should be careful not to forget an art where she looks at herself and is exalted; she turns away sometimes, but always comes back.

I had the good fortune to see at the house of his cousin Riesner (a kind old gentleman) many works, portraits, unknown drawings, all relics of Delacroix. I saw the most intimate mementoes that he touched, as if I were in his very home.

Outside of all I have been able to gather personally from these new frequentations, there is also in the talk of those old persons a new charm for me, which offered me something like a foretaste of wisdom. They always are in the ideal and are so little aware of the number of their days! Here they are next to the little woman who keeps them together, like children at their first quests. Not speaking too much about Chenavard, who weighs less in genius than in intelligence, there is father François who has the most delicate feelings for music (one would not guess it looking at his stature).

Here is the first plane; I am on the second, on the third, according to the days. It depends upon the meetings. When there is no talk I am a little more involved, but then music becomes the only language and then I modestly turn the pages. ... Almost all love it, the younger ones have my taste, the others remain faithful to the old masters, old like themselves. Music molds our soul in youth, and one stays true later to one's first emotions; music renews them like a sort of resurrection.

(1878)

◆ ◆ ◆

Here are the final words which explain and summarize me[1].
The work of art is born from three springs, three motives:

From *tradition*, which comes from the primordial source and constant acquisitions brought by men of genius, who bequeath to us incessantly and throughout time the moral and reflective life of all humanity, whose great book, written in vital letters because they are of their blood, is constantly open before us; in our temples, on our walls, in every work of art truly sincere and felt, and through which we recognize our own nobility, our grandeur. It is through it that we establish the reverence always due to those who teach. And I mean by this all strict friends of beauty, of the ideal, all those who admire and venerate it, from whom a single word of admiration is able to reveal to us new fields of truth.

The whole mission of the teaching profession, Academy, Institute, is understood only in the awareness, that it has to keep this deposit truly sacred, and in this I clearly recognize, in opposition to all contemporary schools, the legitimacy and integrity of its duration, on condition, of course, that the men representing it should themselves be its faithful and strict disciples.

From *reality*, or in other words, from nature, which is a pure means for expressing our feelings and communicating them to others, out of which our own ambition to create remains in a dream state, a state of abstraction and, in a certain sense, of simple palpitation of life which otherwise does not have its own medium through which to appear strongly, entirely, in all the light and innocence of its supreme expression.

At last from our own *personal invention*, from original intuition, which combines, summarizes everything, finds support in the past and in present life for giving to the contemporary work a new structure; a temperament is forever renewing itself in the incessant development of human life whose progress is incontestable and forever changing the means of expressing art.

Those three forms of the word, the eternal word of beauty, appear constantly and fully in great eras when a civilization in full bloom can then try to rise without any obstacle toward its

---

[1]Written in May 1887.

truth. Example: Phidias, Leonardo da Vinci, sacred models who raised art to inaccessible plastic heights, perhaps lost forever and toward which the greatest spirits look for love, prayer and meditation.

An honest work of art will appear only at its hour. To be well understood it must have its moment: one master made his work too early, another too late; it is rare that a happy glory rises freely around the genius, especially in our time when every artist is searching for his way alone, with no other initiator of his dream than himself.

◆   ◆   ◆

A Note on the Type

◆◆◆◆◆◆◆◆◆◆◆◆◆

The text in this book is Amadeus, a new typeface design by AlphaOmega based on F. W. Goudy's Old Style. Goudy's alphabet, designed in 1915 for American Typefounders, has been completely redrawn for digital composition, with a slight calligraphic flavor and classical serifs. The composition is by ASD Typesetting Services of Poughkeepsie, New York, using High Technology Solutions' Multilanguage Publication System.

This book was designed by Cynthia Hollandsworth, and printed and bound by The Haddon Craftsmen of Scranton, Pennsylvania.